Language Arts ACTIVITIES

Editor:
Barbara M. Wally, M.S.

Editorial Project Manager:
Ina Massler Levin, M.A.

Editor in Chief:
Sharon Coan, M.S. Ed.

Art Director:
Elayne Roberts

Art Coordinator:
Cheri Macoubrie Wilson

Cover Artist:
Judy Walker

Product Manager:
Phil Garcia

Imaging:
Ralph Olmedo, Jr.

Publishers:
Rachelle Cracchiolo, M.S. Ed.
Mary Dupuy Smith, M.S. Ed.

Author:

Shirley E. Myers

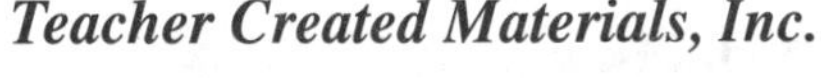
Teacher Created Materials, Inc.
6421 Industry Way
Westminster CA 92683
ISBN-1-57690-349-4

Table of Contents

Introduction

This book contains eight highly adaptable units with lessons and activities designed to encourage critical and creative thinking while building strong writing skills. Each unit focuses on a different high-interest topic from daily life. The individual activities do not require specialized knowledge or experience. Each student can work with confidence while growing in knowledge. These units can bend and grow to fit the needs of the individual student or a particular classroom situation. As you use these pages, loosen your creativity, indulge your interests, and bring your background experience to the table. Your students will be the rich recipients of your leading and facilitating. Encourage your students to look around and take notice of those things that are free—dreams, imagination, and ideas. Let each new unit be the beginning of a journey together.

Each unit will contain many of the following elements:

- Spin-off Teacher Page with pre-writing discussion ideas, word bank extensions, directions for meaningful writing activities, art projects, and lifeskill applications
- In the Writing Workshop applications and student assignments including Today's Reflection and Imagine This!
- Say It Without Words art prompts
- Let's Talk About It discussion page
- Word Bank activities including classifying and organizing, alphabetizing, word search, and student-created vocabulary puzzles
- Think About This analytical lifeskill activities and comparing and contrasting, cause and effect, persuasion and argumentation, and expressing opinions and editorializing
- In the Library: Research, Explore, Discover, Investigate (REDI)
- Student Evaluation and Closure Page

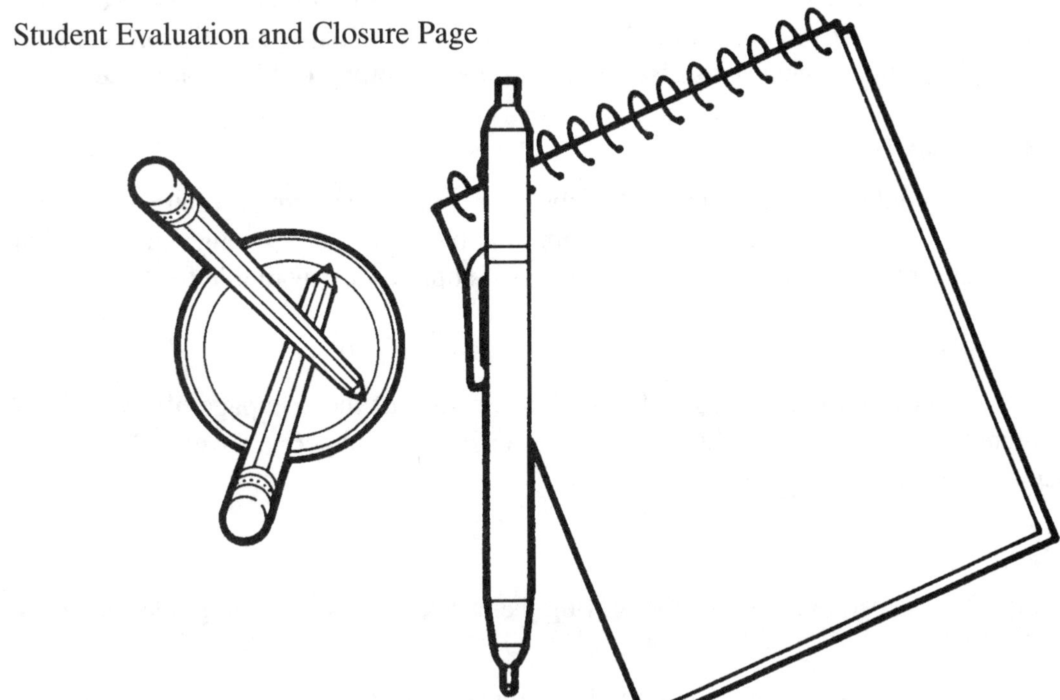

Teacher's Guide Page

Things that will happen as you use these units:

- Students will have the opportunity to use their verbal skills in discussions about familiar topics.
- Students will have a quiet time for reflection (writing).
- Students will learn new words and build vocabulary.
- Students will practice classifying and organizing information.
- Students will learn and/or improve important lifeskills.
- Students will gain word recognition and spelling skills through word bank activities.
- Students will develop non-verbal communication skills.
- Students will have the opportunity to retrieve and analyze data.
- Students will delve into the spin-off topics and think deeply (and critically) about issues relevant to their lives.
- Students will practice managing and organizing time and tasks.
- Students will find new interests that will enrich their lives and broaden their thinking.

How to Use the Units

These activities are not intended to be given as homework. They are most effectively used in the classroom where dialogue and idea exchanges can occur among many students with differing opinions. Students learn from teachers and they learn from each other. The teacher as learning facilitator can provide a quiet, peaceful workplace and can schedule undisturbed blocks of time. In this way, all students are assured of attaining some measure of success and satisfaction.

Reproduction Tips

You may wish to color-code the pages so that you can refer to an activity by color. Use the same color of copy paper for similar activities in each unit. For example, use blue paper for all word bank pages and yellow for all classification pages. This also breaks up the monotony of black on white.

Supplies at the Ready

Your basic "tool-chest" should contain an adequate supply of construction paper, rulers, glue/paste, colored pencils, crayons, markers, and copies of the reproducible grid page, writing frames, and art frames. Students never feel left out of the creative process if supplies are available for their use.

Finishing Touches

Supply large sheets of construction paper for folders. Make copies of the title page of each unit. Let the students decorate the title pages and glue them to the construction paper as covers. As an alternative, students may design covers of their own.

Grading Ideas

You may choose to give a separate grade for the writing pages and/or a composite grade for each completed folder.

Share the knowledge, share the tools, and share the learning adventure!

MY

FAVORITE

SEASON

OF

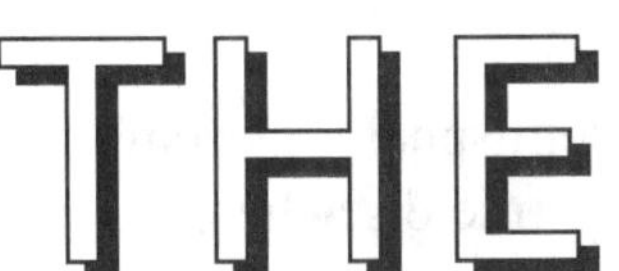

Spin-Off Teacher Page

Pre-Writing Discussion Ideas

1. Read today's weather report in the newspaper.
2. Collect enough newspapers so that each student can have his or her own weather page. If students have pages from different days, discuss the forecast versus the actual weather.
3. Videotape a weather report from the local news broadcast. Play it for the students the next day.
4. If a radio is available, turn on the daily weather report and listen as a class.
5. Discuss how the weather often determines our daily plans.
6. Write the names of each season on the board with a column for each. Have students think of words that they associate with each season. Categories include sports, activities, foods, and clothing. This will create an idea bank for the students to use in writing their reflection pages.
7. Discuss why the seasons change. Discuss what would happen if the seasons were disrupted by natural disasters or human-created disasters.
8. Make a list of these disasters. Discuss the probability of these things actually happening.
9. Talk about how the animal kingdom anticipates and prepares for seasonal changes.
10. Discuss what happens when people cannot do their jobs because of weather-related problems.
11. Think about the types of jobs that are affected by the changing of the seasons.
12. Make a "positively affected" column and a "negatively affected" column on the board and list the jobs you talked about.
13. Invite a meteorologist to come to class and discuss the training that it takes to become a meteorologist. What happens in the typical meteorologist's workday?
14. Bring in weather-monitoring instruments/devices like a thermometer, a rain gauge, or a barometer.
15. Find pictures of weather-monitoring devices and have the students do pencil sketches.
16. Speculate about weather in different parts of the world. In the Northern Hemisphere, December, January, and February are associated with cold winter weather. Is the same true elsewhere?

Word Bank Activities

1. Review all the words in the word bank. Ask students if they know other related words to contribute, and list them on the chalkboard.
2. Alphabetizing is an important skill that is used everyday in school, offices, and homes. Provide a supply of 3 x 5 inch (8 x 13 cm) index cards. Have students write one word on each card and add a definition. Punch a hole in the upper left corner of each card and place them on a ring or a loop of string in alphabetical order. If you have computer access, this dictionary activity may be done on a word processing program.

Spin-Off Teacher Page *(cont.)*

Word Bank Activities *(cont.)*

3. Help the students organize and sort words from the word bank into groups and categories. Identify general terms from the list to use as categories, or ask the students to think of general terms that describe one or more of the word bank words. Write the categories on the chalkboard. Have the students divide ruled notebook paper into columns, using the categories as titles. Ask them to sort the remaining words, writing them in the appropriate columns. Depending on the categories, a word may be placed in more than one box. Are there any words that do not fit any of the categories?
4. After students complete the word search activity on page 13, provide them with copies of page 136, and ask them to create their own word searches. Have students create crossword puzzles using words from the word bank and graph paper or the grid on page 135. Demonstrate using a common letter to link the words. Once they have done this, they can outline and number empty squares. Tell them to write clues for each word they have used. Clues may be in the form of definitions or sentence completions. Exchange puzzles and solve.
5. How many ways are there to say the same thing? Challenge the students to find synonyms and antonyms within the word bank list.
6. Ask the students to identify words from the word bank that have homonyms. What do these sound-alike words mean?
7. Play password. Write each word on a 3 x 5 inch (8 x 13 cm) index card. Divide the class into two teams. Select one student from each team to be the first clue-givers. Clue-givers take turns providing a one word clue to their respective teams. For each clue, the team has a thirty-second response time. The student who responds correctly becomes the new clue-giver. Keep score, giving 10 points for a correct response to the first clue, nine for the second clue, etc.

In the Writing Workshop

1. Encourage the students to give as much detail as possible when completing the survey activity on page 10. This is the first step in organizing their writing.
2. Provide copies of the student writing frame on page 134 for the students' paragraphs.
3. Surveys and statistics are everywhere. Use the activities on pages 11 and 12 to introduce students to collecting and analyzing data.

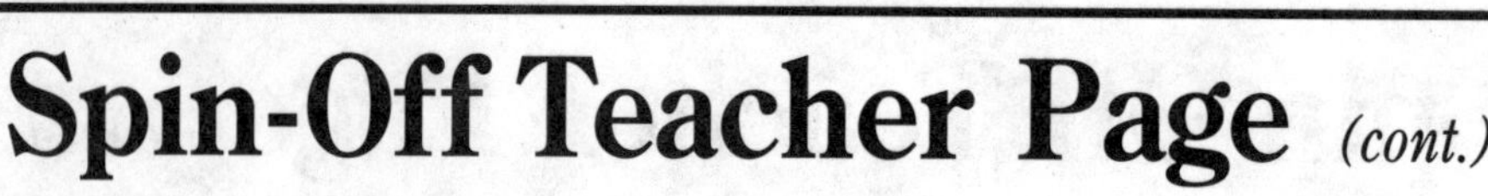

Spin-Off Teacher Page *(cont.)*

Say it Without Words

Is a picture worth a thousand words? When the students have completed each of the writing activities on pages 14 and 15, give them copies of page 134 and the following directions.

Following page 14: When morning comes, it is still storming. You look out the window and take notice of your surroundings. Draw what you see. Use crayons, markers, colored pencils, or chalk to highlight your drawing.

Following page 15: As you explore the island you decide to draw a map so that you will be able to get back to your hut. You want to see everything, so follow all of the trails and even make some new ones. Make signposts for yourself out of materials that you gather. Use colored pencils or crayons to color your island map. Create a "Key" or "Legend" and establish a scale (for instance, 1 inch=100 feet).

Analytical Lifeskill

1. Guide the students as they make their lists of similarities and differences. It may be helpful to move from general concepts to specific details.
2. A Venn diagram may also be used to analyze similarities and differences. Demonstrate one on the chalkboard, using the students' data.

In the Library

Explain that a scavenger hunt is a contest to see who can locate the greatest number of items on a given list. The Internet is a good source of information. See page 143 for a list of sites about weather. You may wish to group the students into teams for this activity.

Answer Key

page 18 1. c 2. a 3. d 4. b 5. g 6. e 7. f Total Deaths: 570,000 in 9 years

page 19 Atlanta, 61°; Barrow, 10°; Fresno, 63°; Houston, 70°; Miami, 76°; Seattle, 38 inches; Phoenix, 8 inches. Thirty inches more

My Favorite Season Word Bank

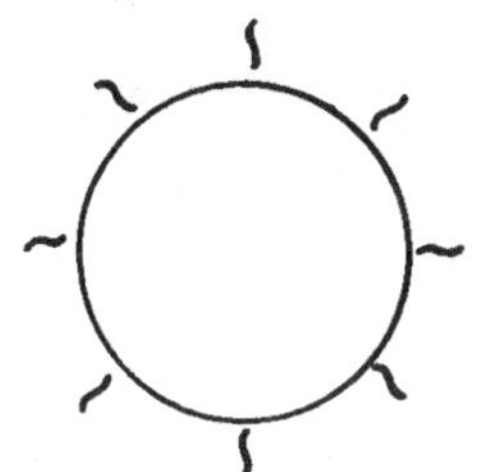

1. season
2. seasonal
3. winter
4. summer
5. spring
6. fall
7. autumn
8. temperature
9. climate
10. humidity
11. windy
12. rainfall
13. snowfall
14. precipitation
15. sunshine
16. hail
17. thermometer
18. barometer
19. arid
20. breezy
21. cold
22. balmy
23. frigid
24. heat wave
25. tropical
26. chilly
27. temperate
28. fair
29. warm
30. pleasant
31. forecast
32. frost
33. icy
34. meteorologist
35. sleet
36. atmospheric condition
37. weather front
38. cumulus
39. fog
40. hurricane

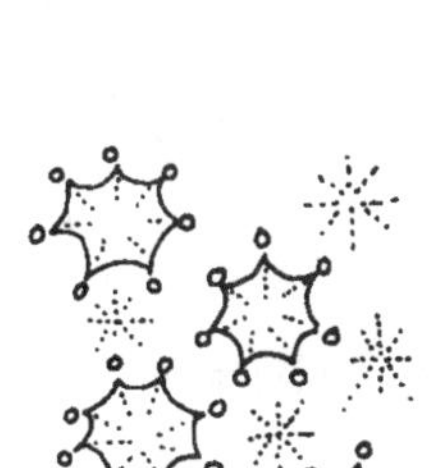

For you to do:

A. What does the word mean?

Many of these words have more than one meaning. Context, or the way the word is used in a sentence, determines the exact meaning. For example, "spring" can mean a season, a piece of coiled wire, a small stream, or a kind of movement. For each word, list its possible uses (noun, verb, adjective, adverb) and other meanings. Use a dictionary if necessary.

B. Using the words

Write a sentence for each word. Make some sentences serious and some funny. Identify how each word is used in your sentences.

My Favorite Season of the Year

Today's Reflection: Most people have a favorite season of the year. Some people really enjoy the summer months, while other people look forward to the winter months. There are some people who enjoy spring or fall as their favorite season. How about you? What is your favorite season?

Step 1: *Season Survey*

1. My favorite season of the year is ____

 ____
2. This season includes the months of ____

 ____
3. I like this season the best because ____

 ____
4. The weather during this season is ____

 ____
5. Some of the things I notice about nature during this season are ____________________

 ____
6. The activities that I enjoy during this season are ____________________________

 ____
7. Some places that I really enjoy during my favorite season are ____________________

 ____
8. The clothes I enjoy wearing during this season are ____________________________

 ____
9. The colors that remind me of this season are ____________________________

 ____
10. Foods that remind me of this season are ____________________________

 ____

Step 2: *Writing Your Reflection*

Put all of your answers together in sentences to make a very interesting paragraph. Give your paper an intriguing title and create a border in the margins that will make your paper look "summery," "wintery," "springish," or "fallish."

Favorite Seasons and Birthdays Survey

Let's Talk About It: Survey your classmates to find out in what month each person was born and his or her favorite season. Interview each of your classmates and record each person's response to the following questions by writing his or her name on the lines provided.

In what month were you born?	What is your favorite season?
Summer June ______ July ______ August ______	**Summer** ______ ______ ______
Autumn (Fall) September ______ October ______ November ______	**Autumn (Fall)** ______ ______ ______
Winter December ______ January ______ February ______	**Winter** ______ ______ ______
Spring March ______ April ______ May ______	**Spring** ______ ______ ______

Favorite Seasons and Birthdays Tally Sheet

Tally your survey results here. Count the number of responses for each season and month and write the numbers in the spaces.

Number of summer birthdays ________

Number of autumn (fall) birthdays ________

Number of winter birthdays ________

Number of spring birthdays________

Number who like summer best________

Number who like autumn (fall) best________

Number who like winter best________

Number who like spring best________

Total number of people surveyed________

Figure It Out

Follow these directions to find the answers for each of the following questions:

Divide the number of people who gave a response by the total number of people surveyed.

Example: If there are 28 students in your class and 9 have summer birthdays, figure out the percentage by dividing 9 by 28.

Move the decimal point two places to the right. The number now in front of the decimal is the percentage. Place these numbers in the survey results blanks.

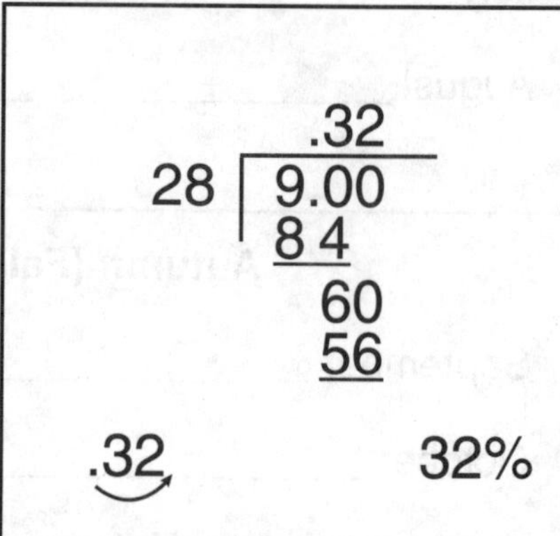

Survey Results

What percentage of your classmates . . .

like the summer months best? ________ %

have summer birthdays? ________ %

like the autumn months best? ________ %

have autumn birthdays? ________ %

like the winter months best? ________ %

have winter birthdays? ________ %

like the spring months best? ________ %

have spring birthdays? ________ %

Question: In what situations can surveys provide valuable information?

My Favorite Season Word Search

Find the 20 words from your word bank that are hidden in this word search. Words may be spelled frontward, backward, diagonally, horizontally, or vertically. As you find each word, write it on one of the lines below the puzzle.

H	R	E	M	M	U	S	L	J	S	L	E	E	T	T	A
J	N	F	K	E	L	L	A	F	N	E	A	R	E	H	W
H	O	S	U	N	S	H	I	N	E	G	B	M	Z	U	I
A	I	G	F	R	I	G	I	D	K	I	P	F	X	M	N
I	T	C	L	I	T	S	O	R	F	E	C	R	Y	I	T
L	A	H	C	T	W	A	V	E	R	H	E	W	E	D	E
W	T	I	L	A	M	M	Z	A	S	T	D	T	T	I	R
S	I	L	I	E	N	P	T	Y	E	R	R	S	U	T	A
N	P	L	M	H	T	U	A	M	V	O	A	Q	T	Y	W
O	I	Y	A	O	R	O	O	W	P	C	M	V	N	U	I
S	C	V	T	E	N	R	Q	I	E	O	S	M	C	R	N
A	E	L	E	Q	A	P	C	R	G	N	U	J	O	C	D
E	R	S	A	B	C	A	O	E	P	T	D	L	L	I	Y
S	P	R	T	F	L	F	B	F	U	I	C	Y	D	B	K
U	S	P	R	I	N	G	D	A	X	A	R	I	D	H	M

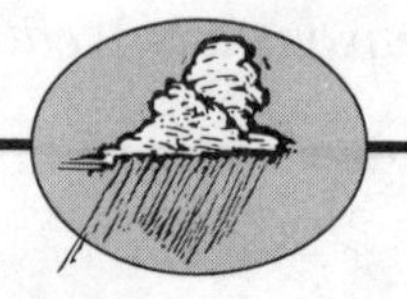

Stranded!

Imagine This! You are stranded in a storm, the wind is howling, the rain is coming down hard, and the sunlight is disappearing. You see a cabin up ahead and make a run for it. The door is unlocked and you let yourself in. Upon entering, you discover that there is no heat, electricity, or running water. Knowing you might need to stay for at least a week, you are greatly relieved to find 10 very important items that someone has left behind.

A. List the ten items you have found and describe how each item will be useful to you.

My Top Ten List of Survival Items

1. ______________________	6. ______________________
2. ______________________	7. ______________________
3. ______________________	8. ______________________
4. ______________________	9. ______________________
5. ______________________	10. ______________________

B. Write a paragraph telling about your week in the cabin. Use the space below and the back of this paper for your paragraph.

Handy Tip of the Day: ***Indent five spaces at the beginning of a paragraph.***

I've Missed My Boat

Imagine This! You and your friends have taken a day trip to a warm, deserted island. The boat that has brought you here will be returning for everyone at 5:00 P.M. Because there is so much to see and do on this uninhabited island, you lose track of the time and when you return to the boat landing, there is no one around. Upon checking your watch, you are surprised to see that it is 5:30 P.M. A note has been left for you stating that the boat will return to pick you up on the next scheduled trip which is in seven days. Before you panic, the note also mentions that there is a sleeping hut on the island with some supplies. You find the hut and are pleased to find 10 items that will help you survive the week ahead.

A. List the ten items you have found and describe how each item will be useful to you.

My Top Ten List of Survival Items

1. ____________________
2. ____________________
3. ____________________
4. ____________________
5. ____________________
6. ____________________
7. ____________________
8. ____________________
9. ____________________
10. ____________________

B. Write a diary entry telling about your week on the island. Use the space below and the back of this paper for your paragraph.

Handy Tip of the Day: ***Be sure to capitalize the first word of each sentence and use the correct end mark at the end of each sentence.***

Making Comparisons

Think About This: Comparing and contrasting are important skills that are used everyday to make choices. Today you may be deciding which toothpaste to buy. Someday you could be deciding which car to buy. Comparing (finding all the things that are the same between two objects) and contrasting (finding all the things that are different between two objects) are useful when making decisions. Look back over your two "survival" writings and make a chart that compares and contrasts the two situations.

Comparing (things that are the same)	**Contrasting** (things that are different)

Conclusive thoughts: Of the two situations, which presents the greater challenge for survival and why?

Library Scavenger Hunt

REDI* Go on a scavenger hunt. Use the resources in your school library to gather information and locate the answers to each of the following. Remember to keep track of your sources of information. Compare your results with other members of the class. Did you find everything on the list?

1. What kinds of weather does the Severe Forecast Center in Kansas City, Missouri, track and report?

   ____

2. Describe the work of the National Hurricane Center in Coral Gables, Florida.

   ____

3. What is the difference between weather and climate?

   ____

4. What are the five climatic zones and what determines these zones?

   ____

5. Where is the National Weather Service located and what is its purpose?

   ____

6. What is the purpose of the National Meteorological Center in Suitland, Maryland?

   ____

7. Find information about or pictures of these weather instruments and describe each one: anemometer, hygrometer, barometer, rain gauge, snow gauge, weather vane, ceilometer, and transmissometer.

   ____

8. Can the destruction of the ozone layer affect the weather and seasons? Explain.

   ____

9. What is causing global warming and the greenhouse effect? Can the weather and the seasons be affected by these environmental problems?

   ____

10. What is the longest (greatest amount of daylight hours) day of the year?

    ____

11. What is the shortest (least amount of daylight hours) day of the year?

    ____

12. If you could travel to any city on the globe, where would you go? What is the latitude and longitude of this city? What season would you expect to enjoy the most?

    ____

Research-Explore-Discover-Investigate

Weather In the Extreme!

Analytical Lifeskill: If you had to choose, which of these extreme weather situations would you rather experience? Don't even bother trying to use an umbrella!

typhoon *hurricane* *chinook* *sirocco* *monsoon*
windstorm *blizzard* *cyclone* *tornado* *severe thunderstorm*

For you to do:

Match the weather condition with its description.

1. blizzard
2. cyclone
3. severe thunderstorm
4. hurricane
5. chinook
6. monsoon
7. sirocco

a. rotating winds with precipitation
b. cyclone with severe winds over 75 mph
c. strong winds over 35 mph with snowfall
d. winds over 58 mph and hail
e. wind with heavy rain in Southeast Asia
f. dusty winds with hot, humid air
g. moist, warm wind with quick rise in temperature

Fact: Look at the statistics below and calculate how many people have lost their lives due to extreme weather conditions in Bengal and Bangladesh (located on the Bay of Bengal).

Deaths

1942	Hurricane in Bengal	40,000
1963	Windstorm in Bangladesh	22,000
1965	Windstorm in Bangladesh (May)	17,000
1965	Windstorm in Bangladesh (June)	30,000
1965	Windstorm in Bangladesh (December)	10,000
1970	Cyclone in Bangladesh	300,000
1985	Cyclone in Bangladesh	10,000
1991	Cyclone in Bangladesh	139,000
1993	Monsoon in Bangladesh	2,000

Total Weather-Related Deaths: _________ in _________ years

For Further Thought

The Red Cross was founded in 1863 and has branches throughout the world ready to assist people in times of disaster. What do you know about the Red Cross?

- Would you be willing to volunteer your time to your community if a disaster occurred?
- What kinds of things would you be able and willing to do?

Figure It Out

Analytical Lifeskill: Which climate suits you the best? The chart below shows information about the temperatures of five different cities: Atlanta, Georgia; Barrow, Alaska; Fresno, California; Houston, Texas; and Miami, Florida. Use the chart to decide on your choice for number one.

Average Monthly Temperature in Fahrenheit degrees

	Atlanta	Barrow	Fresno	Houston	Miami
January	41	-13	46	50	67
February	45	-18	51	54	69
March	54	-15	55	61	72
April	62	-2	61	68	75
May	69	19	69	95	79
June	76	34	77	80	81
July	79	39	82	83	83
August	78	38	80	82	83
September	73	31	75	78	82
October	62	14	65	70	78
November	53	-2	54	61	74
December	45	-1	45	54	69
Total:					

For you to do: First, add each column to get the total number of degrees for the year. Divide each column total by 12 to get a yearly average temperature. Based on your temperature findings, which city is your number one choice?

Rainfall Averages for Seattle, Washington and Phoenix, Arizona

	Seattle	Phoenix
January	5.4	0.7
February	4.0	0.7
March	3.8	0.9
April	2.5	0.2
May	1.8	0.1
June	1.6	0.1
July	0.9	0.8
August	1.2	1.0
September	1.9	0.9
October	3.3	0.7
November	5.7	0.7
December	6.0	1.0
Total rainfall for the year in inches:	_____	_____

To think about:

- How many more inches of rain fall in Seattle than in Phoenix?
- Why is it important to keep track of weather conditions and rainfall?
- Based on the rainfall statistics, which of the two cities would you prefer to live in or visit?

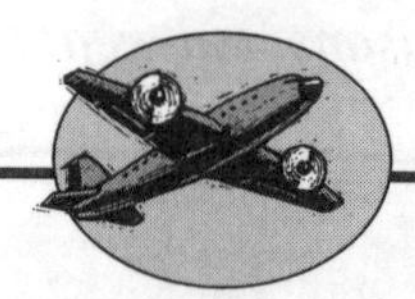

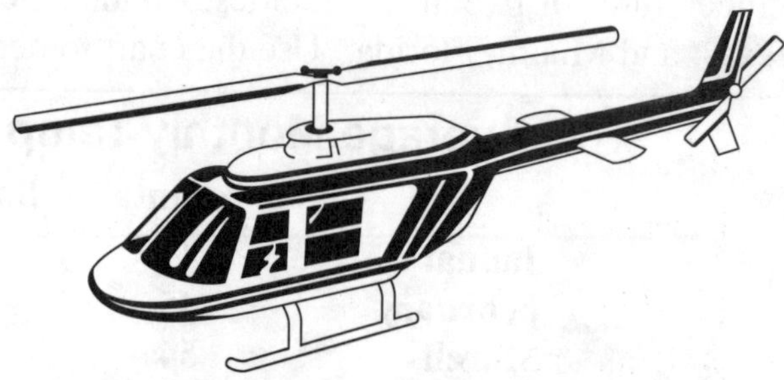

FROM FEET. . .

TO FLIGHT. . .

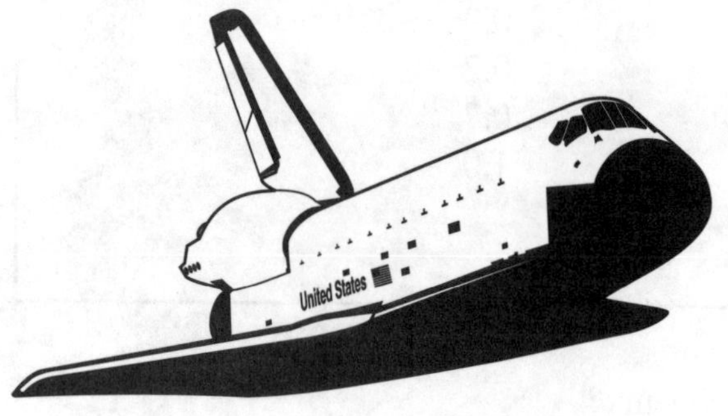

Spin-Off Teacher Page

Pre-Writing Discussion Ideas

1. Make a list on the board of the different types of transportation your students have used.
2. Imagine a time when people relied on "Feet-Power" to get to their destinations. Talk about the limitations and restrictions they faced.
3. Discuss Peter Jenkins' books, *Walk Across America* and *Walk Across China.*
4. What is the longest walk students have taken?
5. How far can a person travel in one day by foot? bicycle? skateboard? train? bus? car? boat? jet?
6. Just for fun, have students measure the length of their feet in inches, and the length of their arms from elbow to wrist. Compare the measurements.
7. Discuss movies and television programs that have travel themes such as *Journey to the Center of the Earth, The Time Machine, Apollo 13, Around the World in Eighty Days, Bill and Ted's Excellent Adventure, Lost in Space, 20,000 Leagues Under the Sea, The Fantastic Voyage, Close Encounters of the Third Kind, The Jetsons* (future travel), *The Flintstones* (prehistoric travel) *Star Trek, Back To The Future,* etc.
8. Have students talk about why people have such an interest in travel.
9. Use a map and globe to talk about interesting trips your students have taken or would like to take.

Word Bank Activities

1. Use a map and globe to reinforce an understanding of latitude and longitude.
2. Provide a large file card for students to keep a "vocabulary travel log" of transportation and travel words and phrases such as latitude and longitude. Use the highlighted words and phrases throughout the spin-off pages as vocabulary-learning opportunities.
3. Have students make flashcards with words from the word bank list. In groups of four, students can play "password." One student draws a card and tries to convey the meaning of the word on the card by giving a clue. His or her partner tries to guess the word. If the guess is incorrect, the opposite team tries the same word. Play continues on the word until one of the teams guesses correctly.
4. Define "mass transit" and "public transit" and discuss the importance of development of mass/public transportation for the future.
5. Discuss environmental issues related to transportation: natural resource consumption, off shore drilling, oil spills, endangerment of ocean life, air pollution, and other issues.
6. Discuss the environmental issue of traffic jams and air pollution in natural settings such as Yosemite National Park and the Grand Canyon National Park.
7. Think of possible solutions to these problematic issues.
8. Discuss trip-planning vocabulary like reservations, upgrades, booking, schedule, itinerary, passage, and route.

Spin-Off Teacher Page *(cont.)*

In the Writing Workshop

1. Have students research the invention of the wheel and then write a newspaper article chronicling the invention and its impact on daily living. The newspaper article should be written from the point of view of someone who lived back in time and witnessed the use of the first wheel. Explain the importance of reporting the five w's in news writing: who, what, when, where, and why (or how). Tell the students to decide which fact is most important to the story and use it for the first sentence.
2. If Cinderella's pumpkin turned into an elegant carriage, what other fruits and vegetables could turn into transport? Write a children's story in which another piece of fruit or vegetable turns into a conveyance of some type. Have students illustrate their story.
3. Have students keep a record of their travel mileage for one school week. Give them the assignment on Friday so they can begin on Monday. At the end of the week, have students summarize their week's travel. How many miles did they cover? If they were to travel north, south, east, or west given the same amount of mileage, where could they have gone this week?
4. Have students discuss and research the Americans with Disabilities Act of 1990 which was passed so that handicapped people would have access to public transit services. What kinds of disabilities would someone have that would make using public transit difficult or impossible to use? What changes were made with the passing of the Act of 1990? How did this affect the lives of the disabled? Write a reflection discussing your thoughts and ideas on this topic.

Say It Without Words

1. Have students make individual transportation collages to put up in the classroom.
2. Locate a poem in your literature book that conveys some aspect of transportation. Have the students read and discuss the poem. Then let the students create an illustration of the poem.
3. Perk interest in model-building by bringing to class a model car, boat, or ship building kit.
4. Have student model-builders bring in their completed models.
5. Have a model-building week and have students spend time each day working on their models.

In the Library

1. Place the names of the following transport modes on 3 x 5 cards. Take students to the library and pass out cards randomly. Students will need to research and find a picture of their transport which they will sketch. Make enough cards for each student. (As an extension of this project, you might want to provide graph paper and show them how to enlarge their pictures.)

   a. Chinese fishing boat
   b. Phoenician cargo ship
   c. Greek/Roman warships
   d. *Santa María, Niña, and Pinta*
   e. British clipper ship
   f. American steamboat
   g. chariot
   h. Conestoga wagon
   i. carriage
   j. prairie schooner
   k. submarine
   l. Model-T
   m. dirigible

Spin-Off Teacher Page *(cont.)*

Analytical Lifeskill

1. Bring copies of local maps to class and have students practice finding locations. Using your maps, give each student a starting point (Point A) and have each of them write directions to a destination (Point B) which you have chosen. Students can practice using directional words such as *north, south, east,* and *west.*
2. Using the map legend or key, determine the number of miles between different locations.
3. Invite guest speakers to talk about safety issues (law enforcement officers, rescue workers, hospital workers) concerning driving.
4. Obtain driver applications from the Department of Motor Vehicles and have students practice filling out forms using good penmanship.
5. Research the driving laws of your state, particularly laws pertaining to young drivers.
6. Obtain transit schedules (bus, train, light rail, subway, etc.) and show students how to read schedules (make a transparency of your copy to use on the overhead projector).
7. Build a classroom library of high-interest travel and transportation magazines. Ask parents and other staff members to donate magazines such as *National Geographic, Car and Driver, Motortrend, Popular Mechanics, Road and Track, Popular Science,* and boating and aircraft magazines for your classroom.

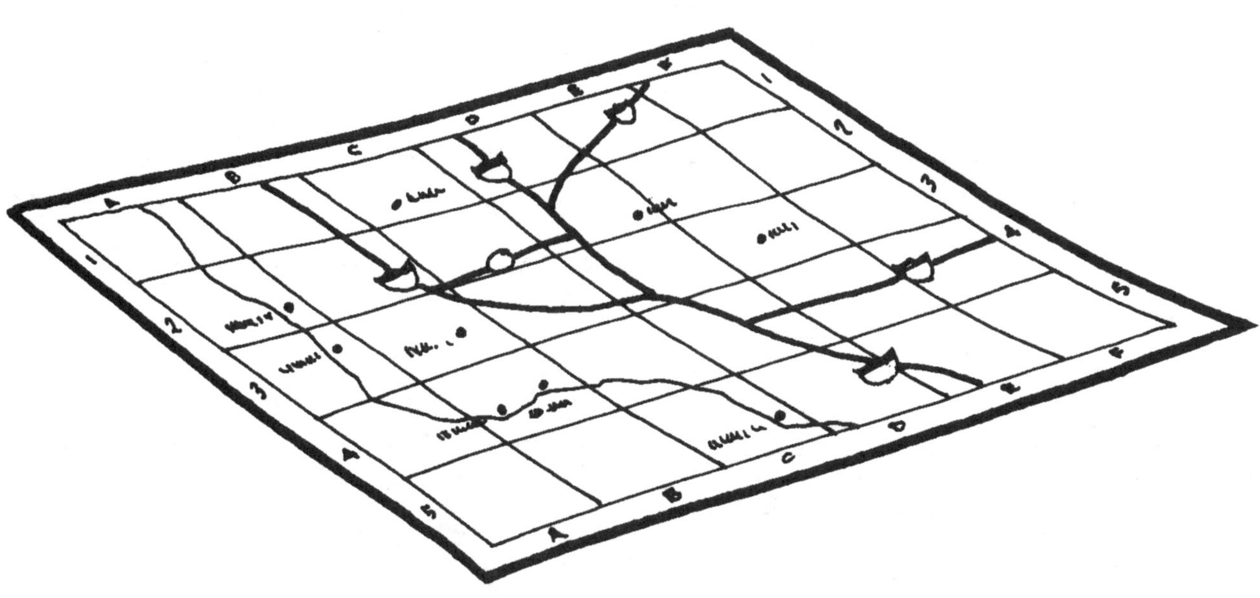

Answer Key

Page 28 1. f 2. j 3. e 4. h 5. l 6. k 7. a 8. b 9. c 10. d 11. g 12. i

Will You Take the Submarine or Space Shuttle Today?

How many of these transportation vocabulary terms do you know? Use your own words to write brief definitions for each word. If you do not know the meaning of a word, look it up in the dictionary.

Word Bank

1. transportation ______
2. conveyance ______
3. cartage ______
4. delivery ______
5. freight ______
6. navigation ______
7. payload ______
8. unicycle ______
9. transfer ______
10. shipment ______
11. teamster ______
12. transport ______
13. express ______
14. dirigible ______
15. tandem bicycle ______
16. diesel ______
17. altimeter ______
18. carburetor ______
19. radar ______
20. transcontinental ______
21. transoceanic ______
22. sampan ______
23. turbojet ______
24. submarine ______
25. submersible ______
26. aeronautics ______
27. autopilot ______
28. hangar ______
29. terminal ______
30. helicopter ______
31. chariot ______
32. supersonic ______
33. galleon ______
34. gondola ______
35. dinghy ______
36. kayak ______
37. catamaran ______
38. bathyscaphe ______
39. port ______
40. pier ______
41. subway ______
42. monorail ______
43. propeller ______
44. hull ______
45. periscope ______
46. rudder ______
47. transmission ______
48. ballast tanks ______
49. hydrofoil ______
50. locomotive ______

My Favorite Modes of Transportation

Today's Reflection: There are many modes, or types, of transportation that we use daily. Some transportation modes are ordinary, like bicycles, cars, buses, and vans, while others, like helicopters, jets, rescue vehicles, and speed boats, are extraordinary. In today's reflection, talk about the different modes of transportation you have used.

Step One: Transportation Survey

1. List all of the different modes of transportation that you have used from the time you were a baby to the present.____________________
2. What transportation mode do you use regularly? ____________________
3. What is the average speed of this transportation mode?____________________
4. What is the primary purpose of this transport?____________________
5. Select the most interesting transportation mode you have used and describe its shape, color, and sound.____________________
6. Estimate an average traveling speed for this transport.____________________
7. Estimate the number of people that can safely travel in this transport. ____________________
8. When you traveled in this transport, what was your destination?____________________
9. What mode of transportation would you like to use someday that you haven't yet used?

   ____
10. Look ahead. What do you think transportation will be like 50 years from now?

    ____

Step 2: Writing Your Reflection

Put all of your answers for questions #1–9 in one paragraph. Include any other information that you would like to share about your transportation experiences.

Begin a new paragraph with your answer to question #10.

Give your reflection a fun title.

Handy Tip of the Day: *When you are answering questions, always "restate" the question. Look at these examples and use this technique as you answer your transportation questions:*
Question: *What transportation mode do you use regularly?*
Answer: *The transportation mode that I use regularly is . . . .*
(Notice that many words from the question are used in the answer . . . this is "restating the question".) Use this technique to become a better writer instantly!

Classifying by Usage

Stretch your thinking and quickly brainstorm as many transportation modes as you can. Place each transport in a classification (group) according to its use. If a particular mode has more than one use, place it in all the categories that apply.

Hint: Be as specific as possible. Instead of "truck," try "pick-up truck," "semi-trailer," etc. Can you think of other classifications?

Recreation	**Rescue/Emergency**
____________________	____________________
____________________	____________________
____________________	____________________
Personal Use	**Military Defense** (Coast Guard, Navy, Air Force, Army, Marines, National Guard)
____________________	____________________
____________________	____________________
____________________	____________________
Public/Mass Transit	**Working vehicles** (cargo, delivery, shipment, farming)
____________________	____________________
____________________	____________________
____________________	____________________

To think about: Transport vehicles can achieve movement with different means. Quickly name one vehicle that is moved by the following:

propeller ____________ oars ____________ people ____________

wings ____________ paddles ____________ animal ____________

wheels ____________ rails ____________ engines ____________

sails ____________ poles ____________

110 Cool Conveyances Word Bank

1. boat
2. canoe
3. kayak
4. gondola
5. jet ski
6. tug boat
7. barge
8. oil tanker
9. personal water craft
10. freighter
11. police car
12. fire truck
13. ambulance
14. medevac
15. fire boat
16. golf cart
17. roller skates
18. roller blades
19. ice skates
20. yacht
21. cruise ship
22. fishing trawler
23. sailboat
24. plane
25. space shuttle
26. helicopter
27. hang glider
28. jet plane
29. mail truck
30. subway train
31. tram
32. trolley
33. cable cars
34. skateboard
35. skis
36. snowmobile
37. snowboard
38. skiff
39. campers
40. buses
41. Humvee
42. tank
43. motor home
44. R. V.
45. sport utility vehicle
46. all-terrain vehicle
47. pick-up truck
48. monster truck
49. submarine
50. hovercraft
51. seaplane
52. hot air balloon
53. dirigible
54. blimp
55. stunt plane
56. fighter jet
57. motorcycle
58. bicycle
59. tricycle
60. tandem bike
61. surrey
62. unicycle
63. cart
64. forklift
65. wagon
66. tractor
67. backhoe
68. bulldozer
69. road grader
70. steamroller
71. dog sled
72. wheel chair
73. monorail
74. people mover
75. elevator
76. escalator
77. rickshaw
78. parachute
79. lunar rover
80. rocket ship
81. catamaran
82. trireme
83. 18-wheeler
84. surfboard
85. baby carriage
86. stroller
87. flat-bed truck
88. hydrofoil
89. livestock transport
90. bobsled
91. toboggan
92. go-cart
93. dragster
94. Formula one
95. stock car
96. Indy car
97. hot rod
98. convertible
99. lifeboat
100. inflatable raft
101. river raft
102. gurney
103. stage coach
104. clipper ship
105. schooner
106. ketch
107. sloop
108. limousine
109. sleigh
110. paddle boat

Fine Feet/Foot Activity

In recognition of our most-honored mode of transportation, our feet, match the following idiomatic expressions with their meanings.

1. ______ *keep both feet on the ground*
2. ______ *walk a mile in my shoes*
3. ______ *walk on eggshells*
4. ______ *foot-stomping time*
5. ______ *come from all walks of life*
6. ______ *the shoe is on the other foot*
7. ______ *if the shoe fits*
8. ______ *jump in feet first*
9. ______ *foot the bill*
10. ______ *feet of clay*
11. ______ *two left feet*
12. ______ *foot in the door*

a. if the situation applies to you
b. don't hesitate
c. pay the expenses
d. subject to human error
e. be very careful
f. don't get too carried away
g. not a very good dancer
h. really fun
i. given an opportunity
j. experience firsthand before judging
k. now you get to have the experience
l. people with different backgrounds

After you have correctly matched each phrase with its meaning, write a sentence for each one that uses the phrase in the correct context.

Example: *People who go to the mall come from all walks of life.*

1. ______________________________
2. ______________________________
3. ______________________________
4. ______________________________
5. ______________________________
6. ______________________________
7. ______________________________
8. ______________________________
9. ______________________________
10. ______________________________
11. ______________________________
12. ______________________________

For quick thought:

1. What does an orthopedist do?
2. What does a podiatrist do?
3. What is a pedestrian?
4. How many different kinds of shoes can you name?
5. What is a shoetree?
6. What is a shoestring?
7. What is your favorite shoe?
8. Did you know that the length from your wrist to your elbow is the same length as your foot? Check it out.

Energy Crisis

Imagine This! An oil shortage has left your area without gas at the service stations. Because of this there will be no public or private gasoline-powered transportation for a month. How will your family manage to get to work, school, the market, and other appointments without the use of a gas-powered vehicle? How will your lives be affected during the month?

You recognize that this situation presents some disadvantages but you realize that the situation might also present some advantages. Use the chart below to register your thoughts about the situation.

	Five Advantages (Pros)	**Five Disadvantages** (Cons)
1.	____________________	____________________
2.	____________________	____________________
3.	____________________	____________________
4.	____________________	____________________
5.	____________________	____________________

Make a list of people whose jobs would be affected if all transportation came to a halt.

	Job title	**Reason job would be affected**
1.	____________________	____________________
2.	____________________	____________________
3.	____________________	____________________
4.	____________________	____________________
5.	____________________	____________________
6.	____________________	____________________
7.	____________________	____________________
8.	____________________	____________________
9.	____________________	____________________
10.	____________________	____________________

For further thought:

1. Where does the gas station get its gasoline?
2. What is a natural resource?
3. Can we run out of natural resources?
4. Name some of the natural resources that you know about.

Figure it out:

If a gallon of gasoline costs $1.39, how much will it cost to fill your gas tank if it holds 14 gallons?

Organizing the Inventory

Analytical Lifeskill: You are the manager of a toy store and are organizing your transportation toy section. You want to group the toys using the following designations: "Land," "Air," "Underwater," and "Water Surface." You have decided to make signs so that your customers can know what is available. Each sign will contain all of the toys available for that category.

Your information: Use your "110 Cool Conveyances" page as the inventory list of toys that your store will sell.

Example: **Water Surface Toys**

canoe
surfboard
tugboat

Your task:

Step 1: Fill in the planning worksheet

Step 2: Make your signs and include the names of each toy on the appropriate sign.

Step 3: Make a cover page for your project and include the name of your toy store and your name and title.

Your supplies: Colored pencils, markers or crayons and five sheets of construction paper.

Planning Worksheet

Land Toys	Air Toys	Water Surface Toys	Underwater Toys

"Fantastic Fifteen" Fact-Finding Mission

REDI* You have been sent on a fact-finding mission and must return with 15 facts about one of the topics on the search list. You will find the facts in the encyclopedia, dictionary, atlas, almanac, or other reference source. As you search, keep track of your information sources by logging the title of the books you used and the volume and page numbers on which your facts (data) were found.

Your Topic: ____________________

	Fact	Reference Used	Volume	Page
1.				
2.				
3.				
4.				
5.				
6.				
7.				
8.				
9.				
10.				
11.				
12.				
13.				
14.				
15.				

**Research-Explore-Discover-Investigate*

"Fantastic Fifteen" Facts Search Topics

REDI* Select one of the topics from the list below and find 15 fantastic facts that you will use for a mini-report. Your report will contain the following pages:

1. Cover page—computer-generated or handwritten (See sample cover page 140.)
2. Report page—three to five paragraphs
3. Bibliography page—citing (giving credit to) your information sources (See sample bibliography on page 141.)
4. Visual element—create a poster which emphasizes or describes some portion of your report.

Topics

1. Transcontinental Railroad
2. Light Rail Transit Systems
3. Howard Hughes' flying boat, *The Spruce Goose*
4. Pilot Harriet Quimby
5. The Wright Brothers and the *Flyer* at Kitty Hawk
6. Burt and Dick Rutan's *Voyager*
7. The 1986 flight of Jeana Yeager and Dick Rutan
8. The aircraft carrier *U.S.S. Pennsylvania*
9. The Air Commerce Act of 1926
10. An air traffic controller's job description and training
11. Automobile assembly lines in both the United States and other countries
12. The 1960 around-the-world voyage of the *U.S.S. Triton* nuclear submarine
13. Supersonic transports of the 21st century
14. How airmail delivery began and the first delivery flight
15. Who was Amelia Earhart, "Lady Lindy," and what happened to her
16. Charles Lindberg, Anne Morrow, and *The Spirit of St. Louis*
17. The German zeppelin
18. Traveling through the Eurotunnel (chunnel)
19. The world's fastest boat, car, and plane
20. Ill-fated voyages of the *Hindenberg, Thresher,* and *Titanic*
21. Create your own topic

**Research-Explore-Discover-Investigate*

Fantastic Facts

REDI* Continue your fact-finding mission by using the resources in your school library to locate an interesting fact for each of the following people, events, or transports.

1. Orville and Wilbur Wright
2. Human-powered flight and the *Gossamer Condor*
3. Charles Lindbergh
4. *Spirit of St. Louis*
5. Amelia Earhart
6. Joseph and Etienne Montgolfier
7. George Cayley
8. Otto Lilienthal
9. Samuel Langley
10. Louis Bleriot
11. Zeppelin
12. Harriet Quimby
13. Anne Morrow
14. Burt and Dick Rutan
15. *Voyager*
16. Jeana Yeager
17. Spruce Goose
18. air traffic controllers
19. "Wrong Way" (Douglas) Corrigan
20. *Enola Gay*
21. National Aeronautics and Space Administration
22. *Apollo*
23. Neil Armstrong
24. *Challenger*
25. Orient Express
26. Hindenberg
27. *Niña, Pinta, Santa María*
28. Piccard's bathyscaphe
29. Global Positioning Devices
30. *The Mayflower*
31. the speed of sound
32. Henry Ford

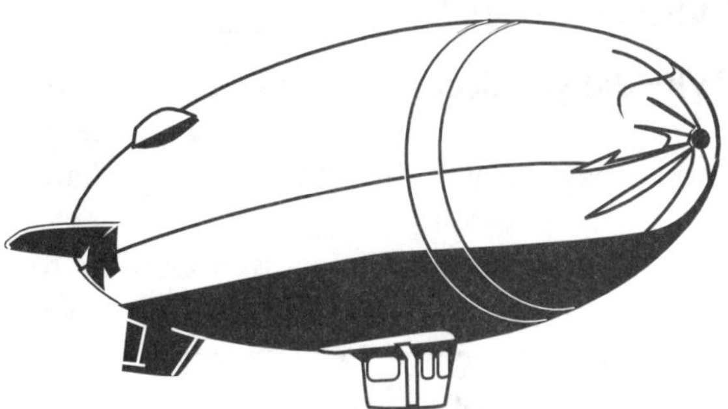

Handy Tip of the Day: *You may not always be able to find information immediately . . . but with perseverance (never giving up) you can learn how to find information on your own. Never say "I can't find it!" Instead say, "I haven't found it . . .yet."*

**Research-Explore-Discover-Investigate*

Time Travelers

Say It Without Words: Imagine that your ordinary school day has suddenly become extraordinary. You and a friend have found an odd looking contraption in the science lab. You investigate the machine and decide to turn on the switches and fiddle with the knobs. Suddenly, lights go on, whistles begin to blow, and the contraption is taking you through time! You have found the famous "time machine" and are now flying forward or backwards in time. What will be your destination and in what time in history will you find yourself?

First, on a piece of construction paper, draw a picture of this incredible contraption and label the parts. Next write a page in your "diary" telling about your adventure.

Where did you go? ______________________________

What year was it? ______________________________

Whom did you see? ______________________________

What did you do? ______________________________

Why did you decide to stay there or come back? ______________________________

Add a page illustrating the most remarkable thing you saw during your time travel adventure.

Into Reality: Begin collecting materials from home (milk cartons, buttons, paper rolls, small boxes, etc.) and make a model of a time-travel vehicle using your recycled materials.

Handy Tip of the Day: *A famous writer by the name of H.G. Wells wrote a book called* The Time Machine. *He traveled through time and had some amazing adventures. Can you think of other books and movies in which the characters "time-traveled"?*

Diary Entry

Dear Diary,

____

____

____

____

____

____

____

____

MY GREAT

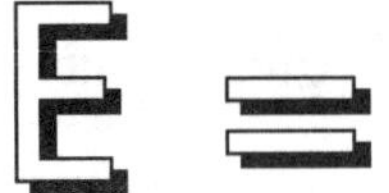

E =

C =

T =

T =

I =

O =

N =

S =

Spin-Off Teacher Page

Pre-Writing Discussion Ideas

1. Ask your students if they are having a "great" day. Are they looking forward to a "great" lunch or a "great" weekend? Were their last report cards good or "great"?
2. Have one student look up the dictionary definition while another finds the thesaurus entry for "great" and "greatness."
3. Bring in advertisements from the weekend newspapers and see if there are any "great" deals.
4. What makes a person great? Talk about the characteristics of greatness and some personal heroes who are "great" people.
5. On the board collect a list of "great" synonyms and "great" antonyms.
6. Bring pictures of the Great Wall of China from travel brochures and magazines.
7. Talk about how the magician David Copperfield made the Great Wall of China "disappear" before a television audience.
8. Talk about the "great mall" in Edmonton, Alberta, Canada. Search the Web for information.
9. Bring in some ice cream and toppings and illustrate the difference between a good ice cream sundae and a really great ice cream sundae. Use your imagination and have fun. This visual treat can be adapted to many non-food illustrations, also.
10. What are "expectations"?
11. Have students find definitions and synonyms for the word "expectations".
12. Does everyone have the same expectations for a specific event? Use examples like the first day of school, a vacation trip, a day at an amusement park. Ask students for their expectations. What are parents' or teachers' expectations for these events?
13. Show a brief video clip of Charles Dickens' *Great Expectations* or read a portion of the text. Discuss what "great expectations" a child growing up in poverty could have.
14. Have students complete the acrostic on the unit title page for the word "Expectations." Tell them to let each letter begin a word that has something to do with their futures, like E=excellence, or effort, exciting, education, etc.

Word Bank Activities

1. Use heavy construction paper or cardboard to make group Scrabble boards. Tiles can be made of plastic milk carton caps by simply writing the letter on the inside of the cap. Tile boards can be made from egg cartons which provide a visual shield from the opponent. Establish some new rules, such as allowing the use of acrostics.
2. Maintain an ongoing listing of acrostics.
3. Have students invent their own acrostics after completing "E-X-P-E-C-T-A-T-I-0-N-S" on the unit cover page on page 35.
4. Students may use their own names as an acrostic activity. Using strips of construction paper have students decorate their name acronym using glitter, puffy paints, sequins, beads, or other craft items.

Spin-Off Teacher Page *(cont.)*

In the Writing Workshop

1. Demonstrate the usefulness of "restating the question" as a writing technique that can improve grades in all subjects and in essay test questions.
2. Students can practice addressing an envelope and writing a business letter of request by sending for information from colleges and other learning institutions.
3. Have students find the Board of Tourism or Chamber of Commerce address for a city, state, or county and write a letter requesting travel information.
4. Using a "Today's Reflection" page, have students write about an adventure or other memorable experience they have had.
5. Encourage students to see each day as an adventure by having them keep a journal in which they record the small, seemingly insignificant events for which they are thankful.

Say It Without Words

1. Give each student a packet of small pieces of colored chalk and a piece of construction paper. Have students make an "impressionist" drawing of the most beautiful place they have ever seen.
2. Cut large pieces of construction paper diagonally from one corner to the opposite corner, and have students make school and college banners to decorate the classroom.
3. Have each student draw a floorplan for the dream home of his or her future.

In the Library

1. Let the students know that each person will be responsible for finding information on one of the "Greats" from the REDI activity. Pass out the slips of paper randomly and or have one paper be the "Great Winner" of the day when you return to class. Have a drawing for the great winner and give a small prize.
2. Encourage students to learn about great people in history and how these people can serve as models. Ask colleagues to contribute names for research. Have students select a name from the list and do a mini-research project.
3. Ask your librarian to show students how to use the Periodical Index and other helpful references; then take a trip to your city library and put the knowledge to use in a large library setting.

Analytical Lifeskill

1. Invite speakers from your community to share their knowledge of travel and adventure. Make contacts through community colleges, universities, service organizations, and businesses.
2. Obtain college registration forms and have students practice filling them out.
3. Use the "Daily Time Manager" for a specified number of days. Have students complete a self-evaluation and set goals for improved time management.
4. Give students a monthly calendar. Begin each day's class period with an organizational time in which students check their calendar for school events, assignment due dates and extracurricular activities.

Answer Key

Page 45 1. h 2. m 3. a 4. g 5. o 6. k 7. l 8. n 9. j 10. p 11. i 12. c 13. e 14. d 15. u 16. b 17. s 18. r 19. f 20. q 21. v 22. t 23. x 24. w

My Great Expectations Collage

A collage is a collection of pictures that you cut and paste onto a surface to create a visual story that others can enjoy. For your personal collage, find pictures that you can use to illustrate your hopes and dreams for the future.

Supplies needed: poster board and art supplies; magazines, newspapers and other sources for clipping pictures, words and captions

Divide your future into the following four areas and think about the questions in each section.

1. **Your future education**
    - In what year will you graduate from high school?
    - Would you like to continue your education after high school?
    - Are you interested in college, vocational, technical or business school?
    - What would you like to study and what is your academic goal?
2. **Your future career**
    - What kind of career would you like to have someday?
    - What interests you about this job?
    - What will this career provide for you (income, home, car, family, travel)?
3. **Your future family**
    - Do you plan to marry?
    - What kind of family do you hope to have someday (spouse, children, relatives, friends, pets, etc.)?
4. **Your adventure plans**
    - where would you like to travel and what would you like to see?
    - what adventures would you like to experience (climbing mountains, bicycling across the U.S., sailing across the Pacific Ocean, flying around the world, etc.)?

Put images that represent your hopes and dreams for the future on your collage, to create a visual reminder of the direction in which you would like to go with your life. Do not place limitations on your hopes and dreams. Let your collage burst with excitement as you think about your future. Have fun!

Your Education Word Bank

Define the following words using your own words. If you do not know the meaning of a word or term, look it up in the dictionary.

1. academic ____________________
2. faculty ____________________
3. bilingual ____________________
4. standardized test ____________________
5. preparatory ____________________
6. intellectual ____________________
7. secondary education ____________________
8. university ____________________
9. college ____________________
10. exchange student ____________________
11. examination ____________________
12. certification ____________________
13. credit ____________________
14. courses ____________________
15. vocational school ____________________
16. correspondence ____________________
17. counseling ____________________
18. registrar ____________________
19. guidance ____________________
20. tuition ____________________
21. scholarship ____________________
22. remedial ____________________
23. administrators ____________________
24. residency ____________________
25. advisor ____________________
26. registration ____________________
27. transcripts ____________________
28. fraternity ____________________
30. sorority ____________________
31. dormitory ____________________
32. kindergarten ____________________
33. elementary ____________________
34. secondary ____________________
35. classroom ____________________
36. preschool ____________________
37. admissions ____________________
38. campus ____________________
39. technical school ____________________
40. business school ____________________
41. literate ____________________
42. financial aid ____________________

Handy Tip of the Day: *The word "kindergarten" is taken from the German words that mean "child's garden". Notice that "kindergarten" uses the German spelling, g-a-r-t-e-n, and not the English word "garden". To remember the correct spelling, associate the "t" in garten with the "t" in another word for child, "tot."*

Correct: *kindergarten* **Incorrect:** *kindergarden*

Syllabication

In the dictionary, words are divided into syllables to help with pronunciation and spelling. Say each of the word bank words and phrases quietly to yourself and count the number of syllables. Write the words in the appropriate boxes.

One-Syllable Words

Two-Syllable Words

Three-Syllable Words

Four-Syllable Words

Five-Syllable Words

Your turn. Look around your classroom and see how many words you can put in each syllable box. Also include words from around your campus.

One-Syllable Words

Two-Syllable Words

Three-Syllable Words

Four-Syllable Words

Five-Syllable Words

Being a Learner

Today's Reflection: Learning something new does not just happen automatically. Work and planning go into the process of acquiring a new skill.

If you want to learn how to ride a bike, you get on the bike, put your hands on the handlebars, turn the pedals, and move forward. In the beginning, you might fall down, but with time and practice you are able to skillfully ride your bicycle. In the same way, learning new skills takes time and practice. Do not give up just because you do not understand something or cannot do something the first time around. Be a learner—and be a winner!

Answer the following questions for Today's Reflection.

1. What is an activity or hobby in which you have a lot of skill?
2. At what age did you become involved in this activity?
3. Tell about the first time you participated in this interest.
4. What was your skill level at the beginning?
5. What did you do to improve?
6. What is your skill level today?
7. Would you like to continue to improve and grow in this activity, and if so, how will you do this?
8. What do you like most about your hobby or activity?
9. Do you think you will enjoy your hobby or activity as you get older?
10. If you were teaching this activity to someone else, what advice would you give to help your student remain encouraged in the early stages?

After you have answered the questions, transfer your sentences to a "Today's Reflection" page and write them in paragraph form to tell how you learned to do something that took time and practice. Give your paper a fun title and share it with a friend.

- ***Remember to restate the question and use complete sentences.***

Sample of restating the question

Question: *What is an activity or hobby in which you have a lot of skill?*

Answer: *An activity or hobby in which I have a lot of skill is sewing.*

Notice how many words from the question find their way into the answer. This is called "restating the question." This technique makes your writing easier to understand.

Have a Great Day

Imagine This: Imagine that you are able to visit any person in the world to talk about something you really enjoy. This person is knowledgeable and skilled in your interest area and has agreed to "mentor" you.

1. Whom would you visit? ____________________
2. What would you hope to learn from your mentor? ____________________
3. What makes this person such an expert in your interest area? ____________________
4. Where in the world would you find this person? ____________________
5. How long would it take to travel to see this person? ____________________
6. How long would you hope to stay? ____________________

When people go on trips, they often have a plan for their journey. This plan is called an itinerary. Itineraries can also be used for daily scheduling. Plan a one-day, hour-by-hour itinerary with the person you have chosen to see. Remember to include meal times and rest breaks, meeting time, practice time, and any other activity you would like to share with your mentor.

---

6 a.m. ____________________

7 a.m. ____________________

8 a.m. ____________________

9 a.m. ____________________

10 a.m. ____________________

11 a.m. ____________________

12 noon ____________________

1 p.m. ____________________

2 p.m. ____________________

3 p.m. ____________________

4 p.m. ____________________

5 p.m. ____________________

6 p.m. ____________________

7 p.m. ____________________

8 p.m. ____________________

9 p.m. ____________________

10 p.m. ____________________

11 p.m. ____________________

12 a.m. ____________________

Handy Tip of the Day: *Try keeping an hourly schedule for a few days to see how you are managing your time. Keeping a daily schedule is helpful on days when you have a lot to do.*

You'll Never Believe What I Saw Today!

Say It Without Words: Imagine that you have gone on a hiking trip with your class and are now deep inside a wooded area. You stop to tie your shoelaces but when you look up, your class is out of sight. Continuing the hike, you take some turns in the trails expecting to catch up with your group at any moment. Minutes turn to hours and you still have not connected with your group. Suddenly, you see a fantastic, unbelievable sight in the distance that you know will be difficult to explain to your classmates. You venture forward.

Draw what you have seen!

Your Goals—Your Hopes—Your Dreams

Lifeskill: What are the most important goals that you would like to reach in your lifetime? Goals can be small or large; they can affect you individually, or they can affect those around you. Reaching your goals can happen with good planning and hard work. Set your goals high because there is plenty of room in this world for success. Short-term goals are the stepping stones to achieving larger, long-term goals.

Fill in each box with at least one short-term goal and one long-term goal.

Goal-Setting Examples

Long-term goal: *I want to go to college.*

Short-term goal: *I plan to turn in my assignments on time.*

Long-term goal: *I would like to own my own recreation and sporting goods store.*

Short-term goal: *I plan to work at the bike shop during the summer.*

Education Goals

Long-term goal: ______________________

Short-term goal: ______________________

Family Goals

Long-term goal: ______________________

Short-term goal: ______________________

Personal Goals

Long-term goal: ______________________

Short-term goal: ______________________

Financial Goals

Long-term goal: ______________________

Short-term goal: ______________________

Just-for-Fun Goals

Long-term goal: ______________________

Short-term goal: ______________________

Travel Goals

Long-term goal: ______________________

Short-term goal: ______________________

Absolutely the Greatest

REDI* Match the column A "Great" to the column B description. You can find information in the reference section as well as in specific books about each topic.

Column A

______ 1. Great Dane
______ 2. Great Wall of China
______ 3. Great Lakes
______ 4. Great Barrier Reef
______ 5. Great Falls
______ 6. Great Basin
______ 7. Great Plains
______ 8. Great Sandy Desert
______ 9. Great Bear
______ 10. Great Comoros
______ 11. Great Britain
______ 12. Great Seal
______ 13. Great Eastern
______ 14. Great White Shark
______ 15. Great Depression
______ 16. Great Smoky Mountains
______ 17. Great Salt Lake
______ 18. Great Dividing Range
______ 19. Great Horned Owl
______ 20. Great Pyrenees
______ 21. *Great Train Robbery*
______ 22. Great Spirit
______ 23. Great Awakening
______ 24. Great Divide

Column B

a. Ontario, Erie, Huron, Michigan, Superior
b. part of the Appalachian Mountain range
c. eagle on one side; triangle on the other side
d. swallows unchewed creatures half its size
e. a steamship that took 5 years to build
f. belongs to the *Lamnidae* family
g. coral reefs of the Australian coast
h. large breed of working dog
i. the United Kingdom
j. Big Dipper constellation
k. includes parts of Nevada, Utah, Oregon, Idaho, California
l. extends from Canada to Texas
m. stretches 1500 miles across China
n. several groups of Aborigines live here
o. a city in Montana
p. islands between Africa and Madagascar
q. once used by French royalty as a dog of the court
r. mountains and plateaus in Eastern Australia
s. body of water located in Utah
t. Native American deity
u. in 1929 it caused 16 million Americans to lose their jobs
v. the first movie film that told a complete story
w. mountain ridges from Alaska to Mexico
x. 1720s religious movement in America

**Research-Explore-Discover-Investigate*

Absolutely the Greatest *(cont.)*

Some things are just simply great. Fill in the blanks and make each sentence fun to read. Be creative!

1. Bye, mom, have a great ______________________________ !
2. She went to the sale and found a great ______________________________ .
3. We went hiking and had a great ______________________________ .
4. He's a really great ______________________________ .
5. Thanks for being such a great ______________________________ .
6. I had a great ______________________________ when we went fishing last weekend.
7. Pioneers traveled a great ______________________________ to reach their new homes.
8. The concord jet travels at a great ______________________________ .
9. Our family enjoyed the great ______________________________ while on vacation at the lakeside.
11. The class received the great ______________________________ on the outstanding student.
12. It is with great ______________________________ that we present you with this scholarship.
13. My great ______________________________ is the patriarch of our family.
14. I enjoy visiting my grandmother's sister who is my great ______________________________ .
15. It's so cold outside that you should wear your great ______________________________ .

Now write your own "great" sentences.

1. ______________________________
2. ______________________________
3. ______________________________
4. ______________________________
5. ______________________________
6. ______________________________
7. ______________________________
8. ______________________________
9. ______________________________
10. ______________________________

Handy Tip of the Day: *Use variety in your sentences and try not to use the same beginning word more than twice.*

Absolutely the Greatest *(cont.)*

REDI* Make a copy of this page and cut out each box. Give one slip to each student while you are in the library. The student must find additional information about his or her "great" and share the information with the class.

Great Dane	Great Wall of China
Great Lakes	Great Barrier Reef
Great Falls	Great Basin
Great Plains	Great Sandy Desert
Great Bear	Great Comoros
Great Britain	Great Sea
Great Eastern	Great White Shark
Great Depression	Great Smoky Mountains
Great Salt Lake	Great Dividing Range
Great Horned Owl	Great Pyrenees
Great Spirit	Great Train Robbery
Great Divide	Great Awakening

**Research-Explore-Discover-Investigate*

Great Inventions: How Could We Live Without Them?

Imagine This: Great minds throughout history have come up with great inventions that have made life easier for humankind. Look at the inventions listed below and think about what life was like without them. What need did each invention fill?

	Invention	Date	What need did this invention fill?
1.	canned food	1810	
2.	sewing machine	1846	
3.	elevator	1853	
4.	telephone	1876	
5.	zipper	1891	
6.	camera	1888	
7.	escalator	1895	
8.	helicopter	1939	
9.	light bulb	1879	
10.	stethoscope	1816	
11.	safety pin	1849	
12.	pencil	1565	
13.	tape recorder	1898	
14.	word processor	1965	
15.	phonograph	1877	
16.	cassette audio tape	1963	
17.	compact disc	1979	
18.	jeans	1860	
19.	telescope	1608	
20.	adding machine	1642	
21.	typewriter	1829	
22.	bicycle	1840	
23.	cash register	1879	
24.	color television	1950	
25.	video tape	1956	
26.	personal computer	1976	
27.	space shuttle	1981	
28.	thermos bottle	1892	
29.	parachute	1780	
30.	X ray	1895	

For further thought:

Every great invention began as an idea. Do you have an idea that could someday be your great invention? Write a brief description of your idea.

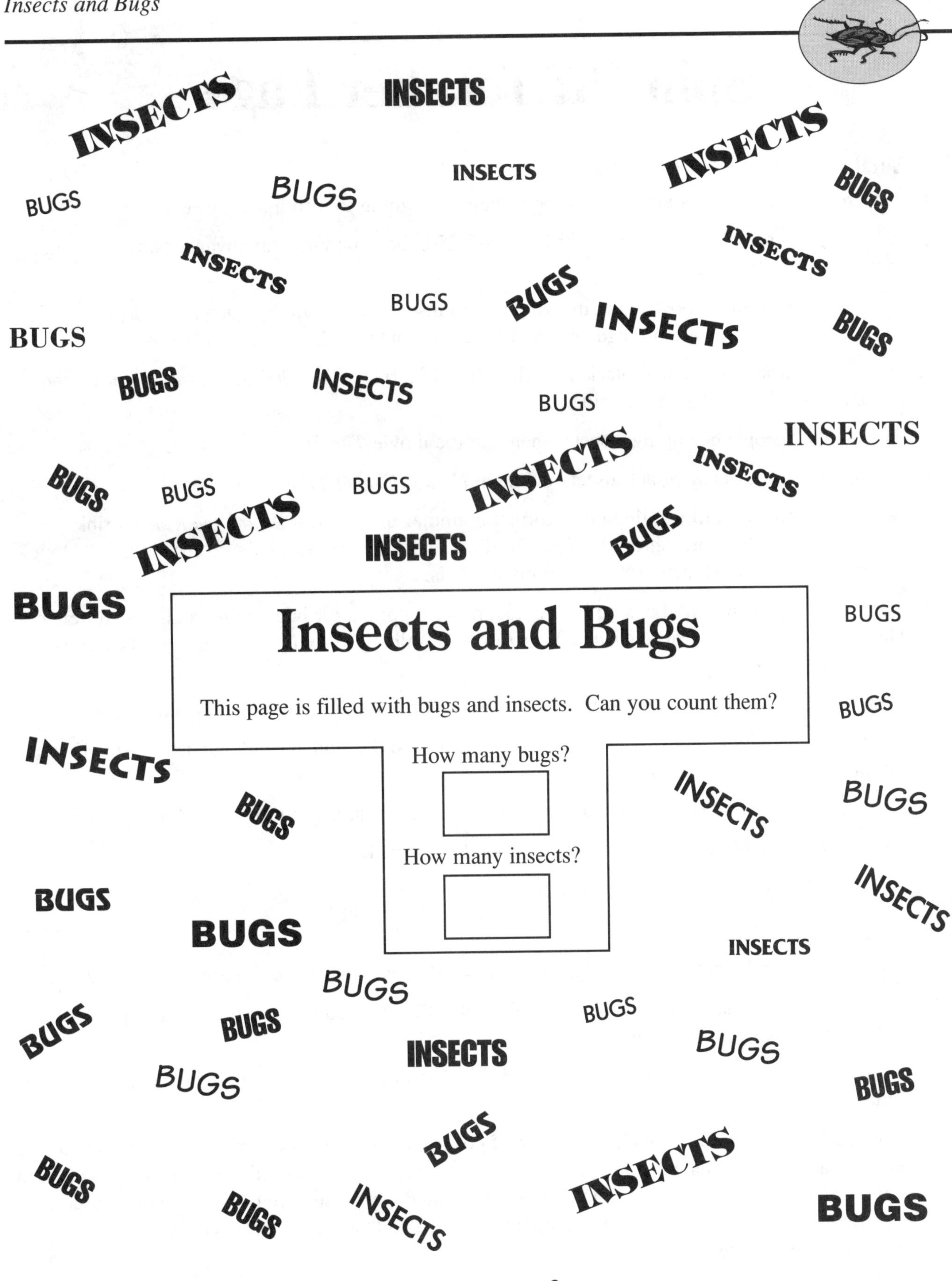

Insects and Bugs

This page is filled with bugs and insects. Can you count them?

How many bugs?

How many insects?

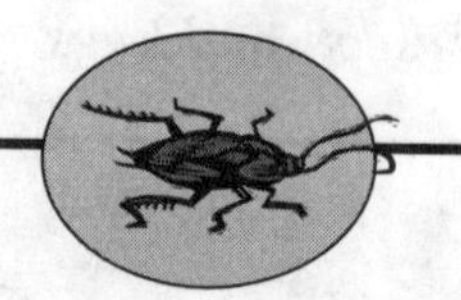

Spin-Off Teacher Page

Pre-Writing Discussion Ideas

1. Ask students which insect they would be if they were going to turn into an insect.
2. Why are insects called "pests"? What is a pest? Use the synonyms "annoyance" and "nuisance" to broaden the discussion.
3. Search for literature or poetry that incorporates an insect into the theme such as *Leningen vs. the Ants* in which the ants are protagonists, and have students analyze the role of the insect.
4. Show a clip from the original black and white film *The Incredible Shrinking Man* featuring the shrinking man's battle with the spider.
5. Discuss the "people becoming insects" theme in the movie *The Fly.*
6. Discuss the "little people/giant insect" theme in *Honey, I Shrunk the Kids.*
7. Do a fun mini-lesson illustrating the incorrect grammar in *Honey, I Shrunk the Kids* (shrink, shrank, have/has/had, etc. shrunk). Here are some examples: Honey, let's shrink the kids. Honey, we shrank the kids. Honey, we have shrunk the kids.
8. Wear a clothing item with bugs on it. Contact these suppliers for bug clothes and related items: The Discovery Channel Store's *Know Your Insects* T-shirt by Gary Larson and the Chicago Art Institute's *Ant shirt.*
9. Set up an ant farm in class and watch diligent ants work. Ask the question "Do ants sleep?"
10. Bring in the children's game *Ants In Your Pants* and have the students talk about why this is such a popular game with children.
11. Discuss the fear some people have about certain insects. Talk about rational and irrational fears.
12. Discuss the topic of swarms of killer bees around the world.
13. Have students find and count bugs and insects on page 49.

Word Bank

1. Use the word bank list to create alliterative phrases (buzzing bumble bees, tiny terrible tick, etc.)
2. Have students use the word list to write similes like "She's as busy as a bee," or "The plane at night glowed like a giant firefly."
3. Discuss the difference in sound, spelling, and meaning of the words "etymologist" and "entomologist".
4. Write each *-ology* word (page 62) on a strip of poster board (one word per strip). Distribute a poster board strip to each student. Have each student look up the definition of his or her word and write it on the poster strip. Have them write any related words they find. Let students present their findings orally to the class. Hang up all the strips so that the students will have a visual reminder of these new words.
5. Have a spelling "bee" using the word bank words and the *-ology/-ologist* words.

Spin-Off Teacher Page *(cont.)*

In the Writing Workshop

1. Explore the science fiction genre and have students write their own sci-fi insect stories.
2. Have students "adopt-a-bug" and give the bugs suitable names. Ask them to write a poem about "Budgy the Bookworm," "Millicent the Millipede," etc.
3. Show a clip of the film *Arachnophobia*. Have the students write about the insect that they dislike the most, using a Today's Reflection page.
4. Reacquaint students with *Charlotte's Web*. Discuss why this is such a popular children's book.
5. Use *Charlotte's Web* to teach a literature mini-lesson on plot, character, setting, and point of view. Give students the In the Writing Workshop Project page and let them begin writing their own children's stories.
6. Locate a lower grade teacher who will allow your students to read their books with younger students.

Say It Without Words

1. Make paper-mâché insects and hang them around the room.
2. Play a game of charades or Pictionary using the word bank words or related tag words.
3. Increase your students' awareness of the correlation between litter and attracting insects. Take your students outdoors and have them go on a litter patrol to clean and beautify their campus.
4. Have students make anti-litter posters and place the posters around the campus.
5. Give students insect stickers as they come into the room. Have those with identical stickers form work groups for creating rebus picture insects.

In the Library

1. Practice researching and report-writing skills by using the Looking for Bugs page.
2. Have each student research one of the following topics. Using the collected data, students may write a brief report that can be read orally so that each student will become familiar with each of the topics below.

    a. the use of pesticides/insecticides in farming
    b. the banning of DDT
    c. organic vs. inorganic farming
    d. disease transmission by mosquitoes and fleas
    e. the bubonic plague in the Middle Ages
    f. deadly reactions to bee stings
    g. migration of the monarch butterfly
    h. vector insects
    i. the dance of the bees
    j. how worms make silk
    k. how bees make honey
    l. how beekeepers keep their bees
    m. insects and the medical world
    n. modern medicine and leeches

Spin-Off Teacher Page *(cont.)*

In the Library *(cont.)*

3. Write the following list on the board and have the students copy it on their papers. Go to the library or computer lab and find out what each of these animals and birds likes to eat: bird of paradise, box turtle, dingo, bat, baboon, badger, bandicoot, aardvark, adder, black bear, aardwolf, platypus, chipmunk, echidna, amphibians, armadillo, chameleon, kookaburra, gecko, frog, gull, coyote, viper, coati, cichlid.

Analytical Lifeskill

1. Invite a gardener to talk to students about natural predators in the garden (good bugs vs. bad bugs). Which insects help eliminate garden-damaging insects?
2. Call a local pest control business and schedule a speaker who can talk to students about different types of pest control.
3. Use the Growing a Giving Garden page (page 58) to develop planning and math skills.

   Have students do the following:

   a. Establish a measurement key (example: 1 inch = 5 feet).

   b. Determine the square footage in the garden.

   c. Decide how many rows of each item will be planted.

   d. Calculate how many square feet will be given to each item.

Answer Key

Page 49 Insects 21 Bugs 32

Page 53 1. w 2. w 3. w 4. w 5. f 6. w 7. f 8. w 9. w 10. c 11. w 12. w 13. h 14. w 15. c 16. f 17. w 18. w 19. h 20. f 21. w. 22. f 23. w 24. w 25. w 26. w 27. w 28. w 29. h 30. w 31. f 32. f 33. f 34. f 35. w 36. f 37. c 38. c 39. w 40. w 41. h 42. f 43. w 44.w 45. h 46. w 47. w 48. w 49. w 50. w

Page 62 1. Egyptologist 2. etymologist 3. zoologist 4. ornithologist 5. morphologist 6. dermatologist 7. neonatologist 8. meteorologist 9. neurologist 10. archaeologist 11.toxicologist 12. kinesiologist 13. paleontologist 14. ophthalmologist 15. pathologist 16. ecologist 17. microbiologist 18. ichthyologist 19. entomologist 20. ethnologist 21. pharmacologist 22. sociologist 23. psychologist 24. geologist 25. gemologist 26. musicologist 27. gerontologist 28. criminologist 29. anthropologist 30. ethologist

Word Bank of Walkers, Crawlers, Flyers, and Hoppers

First: On a separate piece of paper, describe each insect below using your own words. Use a dictionary to find out about insects that are unfamiliar to you.

Second: Determine how each insect gets around. Write a "W" for walk, "C" for crawl, "F" for fly, or "H" for hop in front of each number.

______ 1. cockroach
______ 2. scorpion
______ 3. spider
______ 4. daddy longlegs
______ 5. firefly
______ 6. louse
______ 7. dragonfly
______ 8. mite
______ 9. tick
______ 10. leech
______ 11. earwig
______ 12. boll weevil
______ 13. katydid
______ 14. mealybug
______ 15. caterpillar
______ 16. moth
______ 17. mantis
______ 18. bookworm
______ 19. locust
______ 20. mosquito
______ 21. silverfish
______ 22. gnat
______ 23. millipede
______ 24. walking stick
______ 25. ant
______ 26. termite
______ 27. beetle
______ 28. aphid
______ 29. cricket
______ 30. walking leaf
______ 31. yellow jacket
______ 32. tsetse fly
______ 33. wasp
______ 34. honeybee
______ 35. stink bug
______ 36. butterfly
______ 37. glowworm
______ 38. mealworm
______ 39. centipede
______ 40. water beetle
______ 41. flea
______ 42. hornet
______ 43. ladybug
______ 44. chinch bug
______ 45. grasshopper
______ 46. bed bug
______ 47. scarab
______ 48. tarantula
______ 49. June bug
______ 50. sowbug

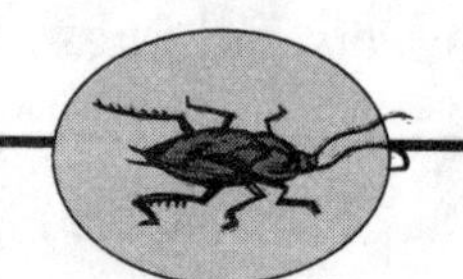

Walkers, Crawlers, Flyers, and Hoppers

Let's Talk About It: Think about the mobility that insects and bugs have. They can burrow deep into a piece of wood or they can fly high right into an open window. List the insects and bugs from the Word Bank list in the appropriate category. Complete the tally sheet below and draw a conclusion from your data.

Insects that Walk:

Total:__________

Insects that Crawl:

Total:__________

Insects that Fly:

Total:__________

Insects that Hop:

Total:__________

Percentage of Walkers: ___________

Percentage of Crawlers: __________

Percentage of Flyers: ___________

Percentage of Hoppers:___________

Hint: *To calculate a percentage, divide the number in the category by the total number of bugs and insects.*

My Conclusion: ____

____

For further thinking:

There are many jobs in which people need to draw conclusions. Name some of these jobs and tell why it is important that the person come to the correct conclusion.

One step further: What is the difference between "jumping to conclusions" and "coming to a conclusion"?

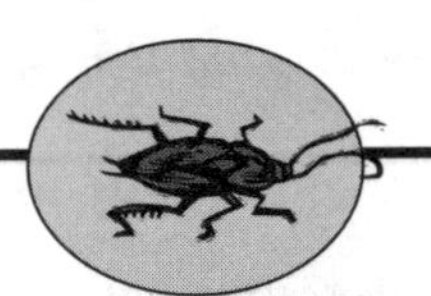

Related Words for Word Tag

1. larvae
* 2. thorax
3. larva
4. pupa
* 5. pupae
* 6. parasite
7. plague
* 8. swarm
9. pesticide
10. insecticide
* 11. nit
* 12. antlion
* 13. metamorphosis
* 14. cocoon
15. prosoma
* 16. pincer
17. appendages
18. pedipalp
19. spinneret
* 20. grub
21. infestation
* 22. anthropod
* 23. vector
* 24. pollination
* 25. drone
* 26. hive
27. homoptera
28. insectivorous
* 29. thrips
30. scarab
* 31. insectary
* 32. colony
33. repellent
34. arthopod
35. citronella
36. predaceous
* 37. chemotropism
38. phylloxera
* 39. habitat
* 40. cochineal
41. coloration
* 42. mimicry
43. ichneumom
44. crustacean
45. proboscis
* 46. antennae
47. chrysalis
* 48. entomologist
* 49. dicot
50. chalicid
* 51. venom
52. venomous
53. entomology
* 54. insectivore
* 55. pollen
56. herpetologist
* 57. ornithology
58. predatory

Note: **You can find these 29 words in the word tag activity!*

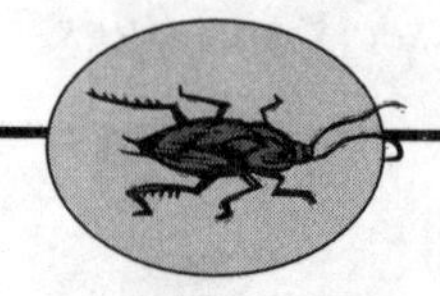

Word Tag

Find 29 bug words on the bugsearch activity below. Words may be found in any direction—vertical, horizontal, diagonal, forwards, or backwards. Some letters may be used more than once.

C	D	O	P	O	R	H	T	N	A	T	V	Y	E	M	H
O	R	T	S	D	J	D	C	K	H	H	I	R	N	E	L
L	O	M	P	T	O	G	I	O	U	R	N	A	T	T	J
O	N	O	I	C	R	Z	R	Y	L	I	S	T	O	A	G
N	E	N	N	O	P	A	N	U	X	P	E	C	M	M	N
Y	Q	E	C	C	X	A	N	I	B	S	C	E	O	O	N
H	I	V	E	O	N	D	H	T	O	W	T	S	L	R	O
G	S	P	R	O	C	W	I	B	L	K	I	N	O	P	I
Q	U	E	S	N	U	H	M	C	N	I	V	I	G	H	T
R	O	T	C	E	V	T	I	Z	O	X	O	R	I	O	A
M	I	M	I	C	R	Y	E	N	Z	T	R	N	S	S	N
N	B	H	Y	K	R	J	X	Q	E	L	E	J	T	I	I
Z	O	F	E	A	P	U	P	U	C	A	C	M	L	S	L
A	N	T	E	N	N	A	E	O	Q	O	L	R	A	U	L
M	V	G	Y	L	F	P	D	A	L	K	P	A	S	F	O
H	A	B	I	T	A	T	H	B	V	L	G	W	B	O	P
X	B	D	W	P	A	R	A	S	I	T	E	S	W	Y	F
N	Y	G	O	L	O	H	T	I	N	R	O	N	A	C	A
C	H	E	M	O	T	R	O	P	I	S	M	D	T	E	I

To do: List these words alphabetically and then find the definition for each word in your dictionary.

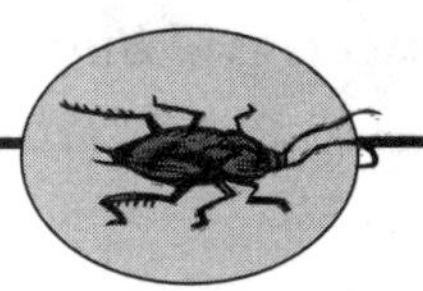

A Legendary Bug

Imagine This! You have spent an incredible day hiking deep in the tropical rain forest of South America with a famous entomologist who is searching for a rare insect that has never been seen by a human being. The local people enjoy sharing the legend of the insect with anyone who is courageous enough to hear the story. Your feet move you forward cautiously and then you see it! An involuntary sound escapes your mouth—you are looking at the insect. What do you see?

Top Ten Questions

1. What colors do you see? ______________________________

 ____

2. What is the insect's shape? ______________________________

 ____

3. How large is the insect? ______________________________

 ____

4. Does the insect make a sound? Describe the sound. ______________________________

 ____

5. How does the insect move? ______________________________

 ____

6. Is the insect a vector? ______________________________

 ____

7. Does the insect have any other harmful abilities? ______________________________

 ____

8. Does the insect emit an odor? ______________________________

 ____

9. What does the insect eat? ______________________________

 ____

10. Where does the insect live? ______________________________

 ____

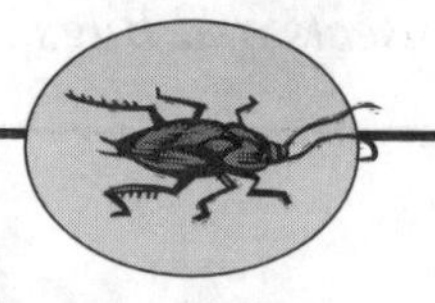

Growing a Giving Garden

Imagine This! Your class has been given one acre of land on which to grow a garden that will help feed the homeless and hungry in your community. Each student has been asked to submit a garden design showing what he or she thinks should be planted and illustrating the layout of the garden.

With good planning, your garden can produce an abundance of fruit and vegetables that can be shared with many people. You may also want to plant some flowers just for fun!

Fill out the form below and attach it to your garden design submission.

Garden Design Submission Form

Name: ______________________ Date: ______________________

School: ______________________ Teacher: ______________________

Grade: ______________________

1. I plan to grow the following vegetables: ______________________
____
2. I plan to grow the following fruits: ______________________
____
3. I plan to use the following method of pest control: ______________________
____
4. This garden will be organic/inorganic. Explain why you have made this choice. ____________
____
____
____
5. After you have harvested your garden, how will you distribute your food? ____________
____
____
____

Handy Tip of the Day: *You will want to do some reading in your library about organic and inorganic farming. Also, look in your phone book for information about food banks and other agencies that help feed those who cannot afford to buy their food in the market.*

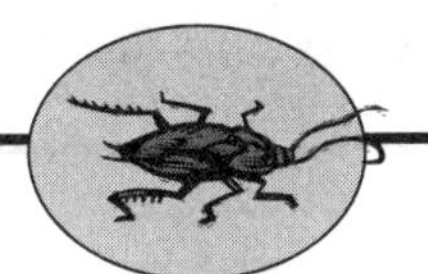

*Hey, Don't Bug Me Right Now

Today's Reflection: Everyday each person speaks two English "languages." We speak a formal language with some people and an informal language with others. For example, some people use a mixture of informal English and slang and find it acceptable to say "Hey, how's it going," or "That's a really cool shirt." Others may find it more acceptable to use formal English and say "Hello, how are you today?" or "That's a very attractive shirt."

Using a Today's Reflection page, write a paper telling how you use language at school, at home, and with friends. Discuss the following questions in your paper.

1. With whom do you use informal English?
2. What are some of the informal expressions that you use?
3. In what situations do you use formal English?
4. What are some of the formal expressions that you use?

Pre-Writing Help and Brainstorming:

I speak informally with ______________________________

I speak formally with ______________________________

Some of the expressions I use are ______________________________

____

Just for Fun:

Write new sentences that are friendly and courteous in place of the sentences below.

Sentence	Situation
1. Give me the money.	(grocery checker to customer)
2. Sit there.	(principal to parent)
3. Do it yourself.	(pizza maker to boss)
4. Give me that.	(theater ticket-taker to customer)
5. Bug off.	(salesperson to customer)
6. Get it yourself.	(pharmacist to customer)
7. Get out now.	(bus driver to passenger)

*How would you say the phrase "Hey, don't bug me right now," in a more formal way which would also make it sound more courteous?

Writing a Children's Story

First: Reacquaint yourself with the story of *Charlotte's Web*, which was written by E.B. White in 1952. This book has been a favorite of children for many years.

- Who is the main character?
- Can you name some of the other characters?
- What is the setting (where does the story take place)?
- What is the point of view (who is telling the story)?
- What is the plot (what happens in the story)?
- What is the theme (the main issue or thesis, such as love, loyalty, courage, etc.)?
- Why do you think the story has remained a favorite of children?

Second: Begin writing your own children's book by selecting an insect and developing a story about your insect. Think about the items in the box that follows as you begin to write. Use the box as a pre-writing activity to help you get started.

Title ______________________________

Main Character ______________________________

Other Characters ______________________________

Setting ______________________________

Point of View ______________________________

Theme ______________________________

Third: Handcraft your book from start to finish using your own handwriting. Bind your book by weaving yarn into holes, stitching, or gluing the pages. Design your own cover using colored pencils or markers to add color.

Book Size: Begin with four sheets of 8 ½ x 11 inch (22cm x 28cm) paper. Fold the paper in half to create a 5 ½ inch (14.3 cm) width. This will give you 16 pages for your book. You may want to trim the pages to make a square book or you may even want to experiment with other shapes (circle, triangle, etc.)

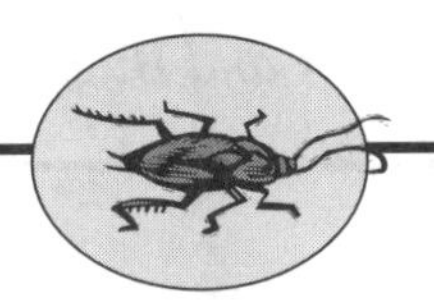

Formal or Informal?

Think About This: Which workers in the workplace usually use informal language and which workers usually use formal language? Fill in the chart below.

Informal language acceptable

1. ice cream shop worker
2. radio disc jockey
3. ______________________________
4. ______________________________
5. ______________________________
6. ______________________________
7. ______________________________
8. ______________________________
9. ______________________________
10. ______________________________

Formal language more acceptable

1. judge
2. customer service representative
3. ______________________________
4. ______________________________
5. ______________________________
6. ______________________________
7. ______________________________
8. ______________________________
9. ______________________________
10. ______________________________

To think about:

Can a person's life be affected if he or she does not know how or when to use formal language?

When is slang appropriate or inappropriate?

In conclusion:

What conclusions can you make about how the use of language affects people at home, at school, and in the workplace?

Use a "Today's Reflection" page to record your answers to your questions. Give your paper a good title.

Reminder: Improve your writing by restating the questions when you answer them.

Example:

Question: When is slang appropriate or inappropriate?

Answer: Slang is appropriate when . . . . On the other hand, slang is inappropriate when . . . .

Just for Fun: Fill in the blanks.

1. My computer is acting strangely. I think it has a ______________________________.
2. I'm not feeling very well today. I think I've caught a ______________________________.
3. There are listening devices in the room so I think it is ______________________________.

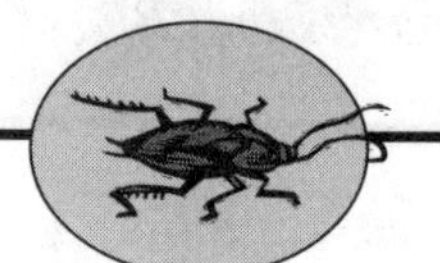

Lots of -ologies and -ologists!

The word "entomology" means the study of insects. An entomologist is someone who studies insects. You can make an *-ology* word into an *-ologist* word just by changing the suffix.

Example: psych + *ology* = psychology
psych + *ologist* = psychologist

Each of the words below refers to the study and learning of a specific area. Change the word for each field of study (the *-ology* word) to show the learner (the *-ologist* word). Match the *-ologist* to the description of the field of study.

microbiology ____________	1. an E ________	learns about ancient Egypt
zoology ____________	2. an e ________	learns about the development of language
ornithology ____________	3. a z ________	learns about animals
ichthyology ____________	4. an o ________	learns about birds
entomology ____________	5. a m ________	learns how organisms are formed
anthropology ____________	6. a d ________	learns about the skin
ethology ____________	7. a n ________	learns about newborn babies
paleontology ____________	8. a m ________	learns about the weather and atmosphere
gemology ____________	9. a n ________	learns about the nervous system
musicology ____________	10. an a ________	learns about life and cultures of long ago
ethnology ____________	11. a t ________	learns about poisons and treatments
neonatology ____________	12. a k ________	learns about human muscles and movement
meteorology ____________	13. a p ________	learns about prehistoric times
sociology ____________	14. an o ________	learns about eyes
ophthalmology ____________	15. a p ________	learns about disease
pathology ____________	16. an e ________	learns about the environment
ecology ____________	17. a m ________	learns about microorganisms
neurology ____________	18. an i ________	learns about fish
archaeology ____________	19. an e ________	learns about insects
toxicology ____________	20. an e ________	learns about human cultures
kinesiology ____________	21. a p ________	learns about drugs and medicines
gerontology ____________	22. a s ________	learns about human social behavior
pharmacology ____________	23. a p ________	learns about emotional behavior
Egyptology ____________	24. a g ________	learns about the earth's structure
morphology ____________	25. a g ________	learns about gems
dermatology ____________	26. a m ________	learns about music
criminology ____________	27. a g ________	learns about aging
geology ____________	28. an a ________	learns about crimes and criminal behavior
etymology ____________	29. an a ________	learns about humans
psychology ____________	30. an e ________	learns about animal behavior

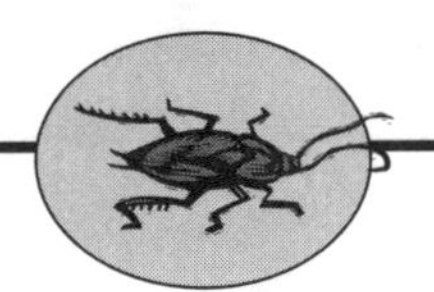

Looking For Bugs

Name ____ Date ______________________________

REDI*

1. In what book will you find the definition of the word "insect"?

2. What is the definition of the word "insect"?

3. Choose an insect.

   List 10 facts about your insect.

   a. ____

   b. ____

   c. ____

   d. ____

   e. ____

   f. ____

   g. ____

   h. ____

   i. ____

   j. ____

4. Write the title of the reference book you used to find these facts.

   ____

5. What is the copyright date of this reference book? (You can find this information in the first few pages of the book.)

   ____

6. Draw a picture of your insect and label the parts.
7. Write one or two interesting paragraphs using your ten facts.

**Research-Explore-Discover-Investigate*

EXPLORATION

N

ADVENTURE

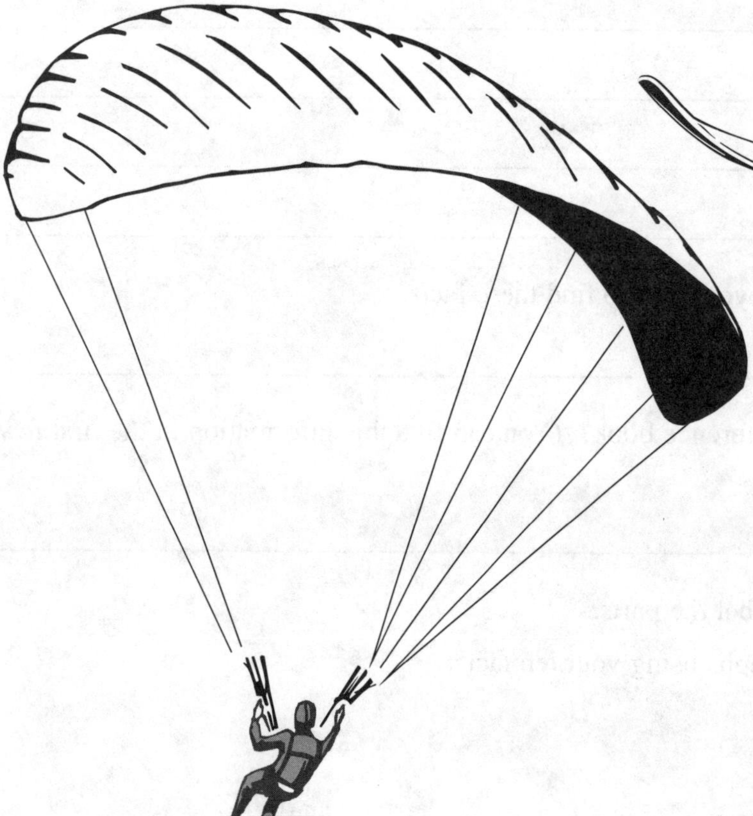

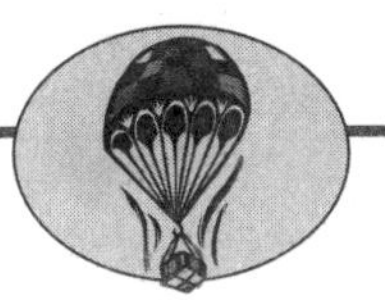

Spin-Off Teacher Page

Pre-Writing Discussion Ideas

1. Ask students if they have ever thought of traveling to a foreign place. Write their destinations on the board and have students discuss them.
2. Take a poll to see where your students have been. Provide push pins with miniature "flags" on which students can write their names. Ask them to place the flagged pins on a map to mark places they have been.
3. Ask students to share the most physically challenging activities in which they have participated. List these randomly and then have students think of possible categorizations (most dangerous, most difficult, most fun, etc.) Rearrange the activities into their categories.
4. Encourage students to brainstorm adventure book titles and discuss themes such as the struggle to survive *(Hatchet, The River, Slave Dancer, Journey to America, On to Oregon,* etc.).
5. Talk about why humans are always reaching "for the stars."
6. Ask what students see as the value of exploration. What would history be like if the human spirit of adventure were taken away?
7. Discuss what life was like 100 years ago.
8. Talk about what great adventures and discoveries might occur in the next 100 years.

Word Bank Activities

1. Go over the word bank words orally, having students write related words as they think of them.
2. Have students select five of the word bank words to create a mini-collage reflecting the meaning of the selected words (Example: The words "investigation," "examination," "expedition," "exploration," and "inquiry" are related to curiosity and the act of seeking knowledge. Students can illustrate curiosity by drawing question marks or finding magazine pictures of people or animals who are looking for something.). Encourage students to stretch their imaginative thinking.
3. Use the word scramble to focus on good spelling. Emphasize how language works only when communication takes place.
4. Pass out a "Scrambled Names" sheet and have each student write his or her scrambled name. Make one copy for each student and see who can unscramble the class list in the shortest time.
5. Have students master the spelling of these words and give a spelling quiz.

   1. skydiving 2. surfing 3. mountaineering 4. windsurfing 5. scuba diving 6. skiing
   7. dogsledding 8. spelunking 9. bobsledding 10. kayaking 11. snorkeling

In the Writing Workshop

1. Have students create new "Getting to Know Each Other Discovery Game" topics.
2. Make a mini-journal to use throughout the year in which the students write the things they would like to do in their lifetime. Encourage students to add to this "life list" all year long.
3. Find pen pals in other parts of the country who can share their daily adventures through letter writing. Have students begin with four to six pre-addressed (home address), stamped envelopes to easily facilitate the mailing process. Keep students' envelopes in alphabetical order in a box for easy retrieval.

Spin-Off Teacher Page *(cont.)*

Say It Without Words

1. Begin a collection of "Great Adventure" pictures that students can keep in folders that they create. Encourage collecting pictures of activities that students enjoy individually, like cycling, swimming, hiking, etc., as well as goal-oriented, growth-adventure pictures such as college, travel, driver's license, car, family, career, etc.

2. Create a class "character" quilt based on the qualities that are needed to be a successful life explorer. Give each student a large square of art paper (2 ft. x 2 ft. or larger). Then have each student select a word from the word bank to write and illustrate. Have students completely cover their pieces of paper with color.

Materials needed: large pieces of art paper, small pieces of sponge, paints, brushes, aluminum foil, gold foil, fabric, yarn, puffy paint, glitter, markers, crayons, etc.

Possible qualities: perseverance, endurance, fortitude, tenacity, stamina, energy, strength, bravery, confidence, boldness, determination, persistence, tirelessness, etc. Have students add other qualities to their pages. Tape all of the pages together to make a class mural and display it.

In the Library

1. Have students select one of the following areas of exploration: science, medicine, geography, outer space, deep sea. Make the extra-credit page available for a personal "I-Search" paper. Have students present their findings orally to extend learning.

2. Emphasize that library activities help students "learn how to learn." Strengthen library usage skills in order to foster independence and self-reliance. With opportunities for library usage students will begin to feel comfortable searching for information.

Answer Key

Page 69 1. quest 2. risk 3. energy 4. brave 5. stouthearted 6. journey 7. endurance 8. goal 9. trailblazer 10. expedition 1. stamina 12. tireless 13. courageous 14. fearless 15. determination 16. purposeful. 17. explore 18 passage 19. endeavor 20. confident 21. *Endeavor* 22. investigate 23. tenacity 24. trailblazer 25. audacious 26. exciting 27. mission 28. pioneer 29. *Enterprise* 30. adventuresome

Page 70 1. track and field 2. baseball 3. auto racing 4. track and field 5. basketball 6. football 7. swimming 8. soccer 9. golf 10. football 11. auto racing 12. baseball 13. ice skating 14. baseball 15. Track and field 16. basketball 17. baseball 18. baseball/football 19. baseball 20. ice skating 21. ice skating 22. swimming 23. ice skating 24. cycling 25. golf 26. ice hockey 27. football 28. basketball 29. auto racing 30. baseball 31. baseball 32. tennis 33. basketball 34. baseball 35. ice skating

Bonus: Johnny Weismuller

Explorers and Adventurers

Many of the adventure-explorer words below have related words that you can make by adding or changing a prefix or suffix. Stretch your vocabulary and see how many related words you can write. Check the dictionary to be sure that the new words are really used.

Related Word

1. courage ___courageous___
2. tenacious ______
3. risk ______
4. endure ______
5. mettle ______
6. fortitude ______
7. resolute ______
8. persevere ______
9. stamina ______
10. purposeful ______
11. energy ______
12. power ______
13. strength ______
14. adventure ______
15. audacious ______
16. stalwart ______
17. brave ______
18. confident ______
19. undertaking ______
20. enterprise ______
21. excite ______
22. bold ______
23. attempt ______
24. adventure ______
25. challenge ______
26. fearless ______
27. firm ______
28. determine ______
29. endeavor ______
30. quest ______
31. aim ______
32. goal ______
33. venture ______
34. journey ______
35. traverse ______
36. globetrot ______
37. valiant ______
38. inquire ______
39. passage ______
40. investigate ______
41. examine ______
42. search ______
43. discover ______
44. expedition ______
45. explore ______
46. pioneer ______
47. trailblazer ______
48. pathfinder ______
49. stubborn ______
50. persist ______
51. trek ______
52. mission ______
53. tireless ______
54. stouthearted ______
55. voyage ______

Double Your Vocabulary, Double Your Fun

Word Bank Activity It's easy to build your vocabulary by taking words you already know and forming related words by simply adding a suffix. If you add the suffix *-tion, -ion,* or *-ment* to a verb (action), the verb becomes a noun (person, place, thing or idea).

For example:

determine (verb): The coaches will *determine* the starting lineup.

determination (noun): The coaches have made a *determination* about the starting lineup.

For you to do: Write a sentence for each of the following verbs. Change the verbs into nouns and write new sentences.

1. investigate ____________________
2. ____________________

1. explore ____________________
2. ____________________

1. accomplish ____________________
2. ____________________

1. celebrate ____________________
2. ____________________

1. cancel ____________________
2. ____________________

1. measure ____________________
2. ____________________

1. declare ____________________
2. ____________________

1. place ____________________
2. ____________________

1. except ____________________
2. ____________________

1. abbreviate ____________________
2. ____________________

1. adjust ____________________
2. ____________________

1. interrupt ____________________
2. ____________________

1. interrogate ____________________
2. ____________________

1. excite ____________________
2. ____________________

1. hesitate ____________________
2. ____________________

Handy Tip of the Day: *You will need to drop the* **e** *at the end of verbs before you add the suffix* **-ion**. *Some words will need an* **a** *before you add the suffix* **-tion**. *Check your dictionary for final spellings. Take note: declare* **-e +a +tion** *= declaration*

Unscramble the Word Bank Words

Each word begins with the correct first letter. Enjoy the helpful *cuel.* Write the correctly spelled word in the space after each sentence.

1. The crew was on a *quste.*
2. Explorers take many *rsisk.*
3. Mountain climbers have a lot of *ergyne.*
4. In the face of danger, be *barve.*
5. The pioneers were *steuothderta.*
6. Columbus went on a long *juoneyr.*
7. Going on a space shuttle mission requires *euranencd.*
8. Every explorer has a *gloa* he or she hopes to reach.
9. Dr. Barnard was a *tlriazblare* in the field of heart surgery.
10. Sir Edmund Hillary went on an amazing *epdxetinoi* to the summit of Mount Everest.
11. Florence Nightingale and her nurses worked long hours and needed much *satmina.*
12. When Peter Jenkins walked across America, he was *tlsserie.*
13. Rosa Park made a *cuorsuoega* statement when she refused to sit in the back of the bus.
14. People who walk on tightropes without a net are *faelrsse.*
15. Louis Pasteur worked with great *dtereimanitno* to find a way to kill microorganisms in food and drinks.
16. The explorers were *poserupluf* as they set out to reach their goals.
17. Deep-sea divers like to *epoxlre* the ocean's mysteries.
18. Many sailing expeditions did not have safe *psasega.*
19. John Glenn's first flight into space was a courageous *eavdnero.*
20. Skydivers must be very *cidnoftne* in their parachutes.
21. One of the space shuttles is called the *Eendarov.*
22. Would you ever like to *ientvaegitse* underwater caves?
23. Olympic athletes must have *tyetnica* because they never give up trying to win.
24. Jackie Robinson was a *treziarlalb* in the history of baseball.
25. The pioneers must have been bold and *asuoiudac.*
26. Traveling to a new place is always *egnxiitc.*
27. Many of the early explorers were on a *mnossii* to find gold.
28. Do you think you would have enjoyed being a *prneeoi* in the early days of our country?
29. Star Trek fans enjoy watching the adventures of the crew on the *Eeesirntrp.*
30. Lewis and Clark were an *aemosdvenerut* team as they made their way to the Oregon coast.

Sports Matching Quiz

Many people have turned their interest in sports into an adventure! Match the athlete with his or her sport. If you do not know who a person is, take a good guess. After you have corrected your quiz, tally your points and see which award you have earned.

Sports

basketball	**baseball**	**football**	**ice skating**	**auto racing**	**ice hockey**
swimming	**golf**	**tennis**	**cycling**	**track and field**	**soccer**

Athletes

1. Florence Griffith-Joyner ______________
2. Ken Griffey, Jr. ______________
3. Richard Petty ______________
4. Jesse Owens ______________
5. Shaquille O'Neal ______________
6. Steve Young ______________
7. Johnny Weismuller ______________
8. Pele ______________
9. Nancy Lopez ______________
10. Joe Montana ______________
11. Al Unser ______________
12. Babe Ruth ______________
13. Kristi Yamaguchi ______________
14. Nolan Ryan ______________
15. Wilma Rudolph ______________
16. Pete Maravich ______________
17. Mickey Mantle ______________
18. Bo Jackson ______________
19. Orel Hershiser ______________
20. Eric Heiden ______________
21. Tara Lipinski ______________
22. Mark Spitz ______________
23. Peggy Flemming ______________
24. Greg LeMond ______________
25. Tiger Woods ______________
26. Wayne Gretzsky ______________
27. John Elway ______________
28. Julius Erving ______________
29. Emerson Fittipaldi ______________
30. Lou Gehrig ______________
31. Johnny Bench ______________
32. Arthur Ashe ______________
33. Larry Bird ______________
34. Hank Aaron ______________
35. Brian Boitano ______________

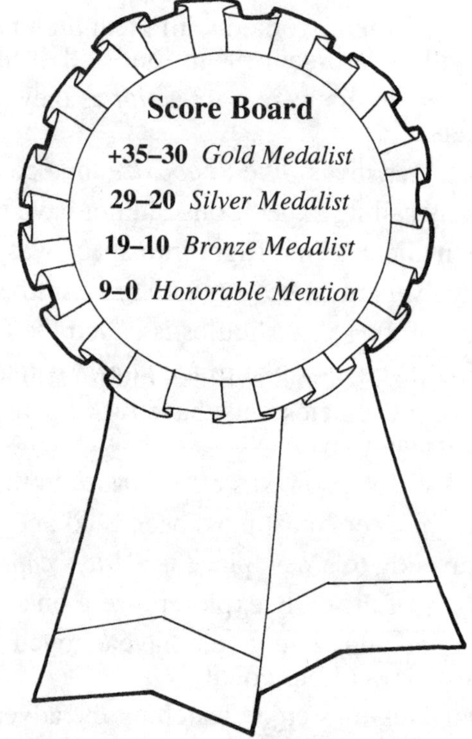

Bonus question: Which athlete won gold medals for swimming at the 1924 and 1928 Olympics and then went on to become Tarzan in films?

Personal Inventory of Skills and Abilities

Let's Talk About It: Since the day you were born, you have been on an adventure as you explore this planet. At first, your accomplishments were based on survival needs like feeding yourself, walking, and talking. As you grew older, you expanded your abilities to include educational and recreational accomplishments like reading, writing, swimming, and bike riding.

Now take a personal inventory of your skills and abilities. Do not overlook the smaller accomplishments—for example, tying your shoes. Enjoy your larger achievements, too.

These are the skills and abilities that I already have.

1. ______________________________
2. ______________________________
3. ______________________________
4. ______________________________
5. ______________________________
6. ______________________________
7. ______________________________
8. ______________________________
9. ______________________________
10. ______________________________
11. ______________________________
12. ______________________________
13. ______________________________
14. ______________________________
15. ______________________________
16. ______________________________
17. ______________________________
18. ______________________________
19. ______________________________
20. ______________________________

These are the skill and abilities I hope to have in the future.

1. ______________________________
2. ______________________________
3. ______________________________
4. ______________________________
5. ______________________________
6. ______________________________
7. ______________________________
8. ______________________________
9. ______________________________
10. ______________________________

Getting to Know Each Other

Let's Talk About It: Now that you have identified your own skills and abilities on the Personal Inventory page, find out what other members of your class can do. Find two people who have the skill listed in the box. Do not use the same person more than twice.

Can ride a bike 1. 2.	**Can bake a cake** 1. 2.
Can swim 1. 2.	**Can fix a tire** 1. 2.
Can play a musical instrument 1. 2.	**Can program a VCR** 1. 2.
Can speak more than one language 1. 2.	**Can iron a shirt** 1. 2.
Can climb a mountain 1. 2.	**Can send e-mail** 1. 2.
Can train a pet 1. 2.	**Can plant a garden** 1. 2.
Can perform in public (sing, act, dance) 1. 2.	**Can play a sport** 1. 2.
Can cook a meal 1. 2.	**Can bait a line and fish** 1. 2.
Can sew 1. 2.	**Can ice skate** 1. 2.

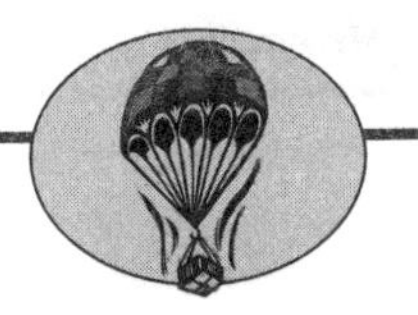

Adventures in Sports

Let's Talk About It: The world of sports and athletics offers many opportunities for fun and adventure. See how many sports you can name.

Name That Sport

1. ______________________
2. ______________________
3. ______________________
4. ______________________
5. ______________________
6. ______________________
7. ______________________
8. ______________________
9. ______________________
10. ______________________

Have you been a player, spectator, or neither?

Now that you have identified some sports, list them in the order of your interest with number one being your favorite and number ten your least favorite. (If you are not a sports enthusiast, use the space below to alphabetize your list.)

1. ______________________
2. ______________________
3. ______________________
4. ______________________
5. ______________________
6. ______________________
7. ______________________
8. ______________________
9. ______________________
10. ______________________

Think about it:

1. What do you like most about your number one and two sports?

   ____

   ____

2. What do you dislike most about your number nine and ten sports?

   ____

   ____

3. Why do you think that sports are or are not important in our daily lives?

   ____

   ____

My Virtual Adventure

Today's Reflection: Go on a virtual adventure trip to a place you have never seen, to do something you have never done. Perhaps you would like to go to France and fly on a trapeze in the circus. Or would you rather go to Louisiana to hunt for alligators? How about snorkeling in the coral reefs of Australia? Stretch your imagination. Enjoy your adventure!

First, think. . .

1. Where are you going for your great adventure? ____________________
2. Why have you chosen this destination for your adventure? ____________________
   ____
3. How will you get there?____________________
4. What will you take?____________________
5. Who is going with you?____________________
6. How long are you going to stay?____________________
7. What are you going to do on your great adventure?____________________

Now, write your virtual adventure story in the box below. You may write in the large box or create smaller boxes for different parts of your story. Enjoy your trip!

Adventures in the Deep Sea

Imagine This! Many writers have been fascinated with the unknown world of the deep sea. The writer Jules Verne wrote about sea monsters in his book *20,000 Leagues Under the Sea.* In his book, *Jaws,* author Peter Benchley wrote about another sea monster. Some people believe that a sea monster (named "Nessie") lives in the water of Loch Ness in Scotland.

What do you believe lives in the dark, unexplored waters on our planet? Imagine that you are a photographer and you have just spotted a sea creature that has never been seen by the human eye. Draw your sea creature and its surroundings!

Use this thinking diagram to help you get started.

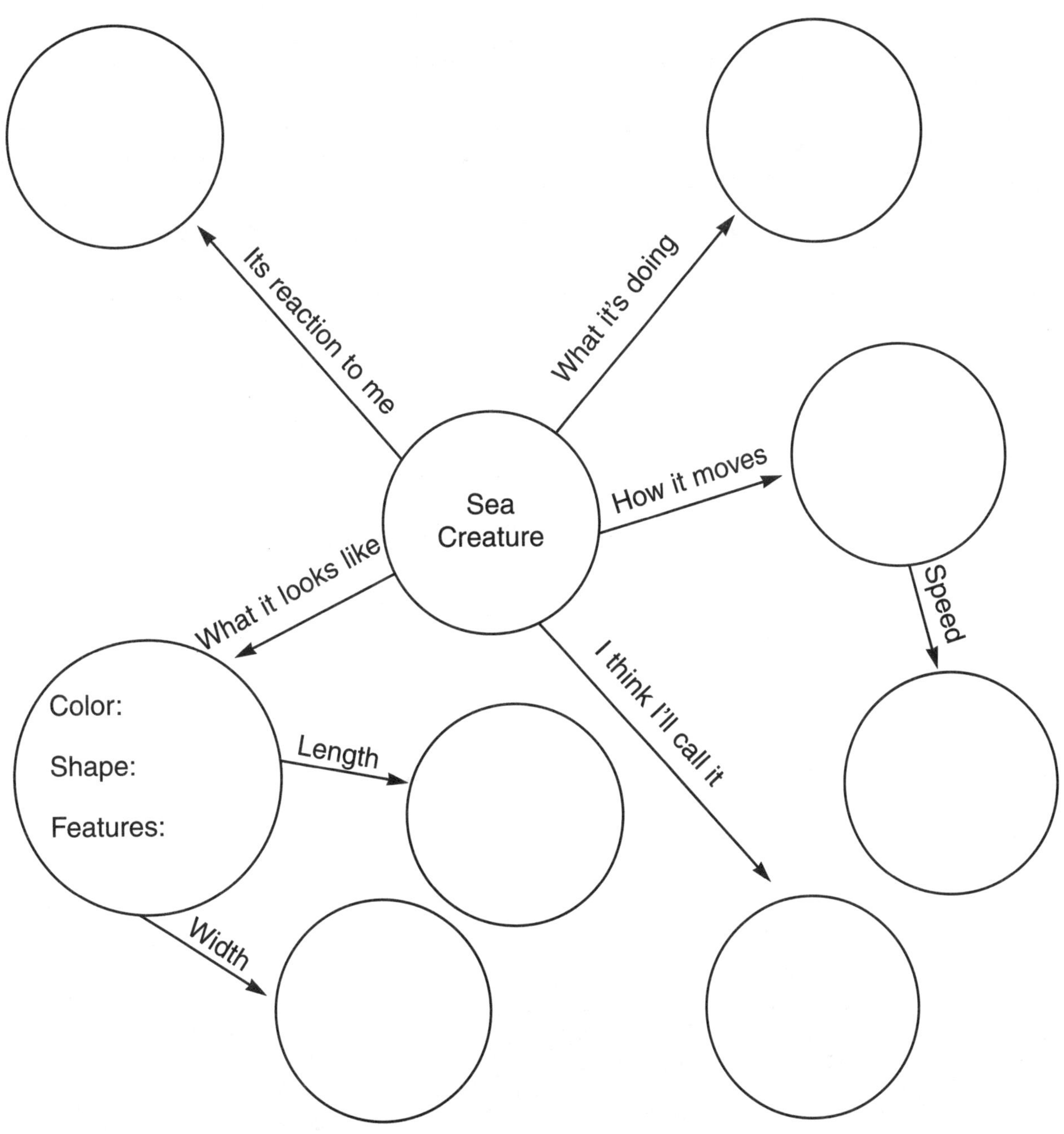

Say It Again, Sam

You can learn to vary your sentences by saying them in different ways. Notice how the same snorkeling message is conveyed but in three variations.

Example:

I love snorkeling in the deep, warm waters of Australia.
Snorkeling in the deep, warm waters of Australia, is something that I love.
In the deep, warm waters of Australia, I love to snorkel.

*Notice how the subject *I* and the verb *love* find new positions in each sentence. Try sentence variations using the following word prompts:

A. **auto racing**

1. ______________________
2. ______________________
3. ______________________

B. **camping**

1. ______________________
2. ______________________
3. ______________________

C. **sailing**

1. ______________________
2. ______________________
3. ______________________

D. **skydiving**

1. ______________________
2. ______________________
3. ______________________

E. **skiing**

1. ______________________
2. ______________________
3. ______________________

F. **deep-sea diving**

1. ______________________
2. ______________________
3. ______________________

G. **windsurfing**

1. ______________________
2. ______________________
3. ______________________

H. **hiking**

1. ______________________
2. ______________________
3. ______________________

Handy Tip of the Day: *The subject of a sentence can be at the beginning, in the middle, or at the end of a sentence.*

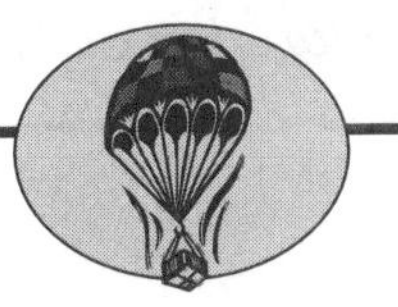

Finders of the Lost Art

Let's Talk About It: Before the invention of movie theaters, television, and home videos, people heard adventure stories from traveling storytellers who held the audience's attention for hours! It took much perseverance, practice, and stamina to become a professional storyteller. With the invention of the radio, audiences became loyal listeners of their favorite mystery, drama, or comedy hour. However, verbal storytelling became a lost art when movies became popular. People did not have to listen as closely because they could see what was happening on the screen.

Fortunately, you have been sent on an expedition to find the "Lost Art of Storytelling" and you have come back with the story of an amazing superhero.

Your Challenge: Create a new superhero and write a story of his or her exploits. Use the pre-writing diagram below to help you get started.

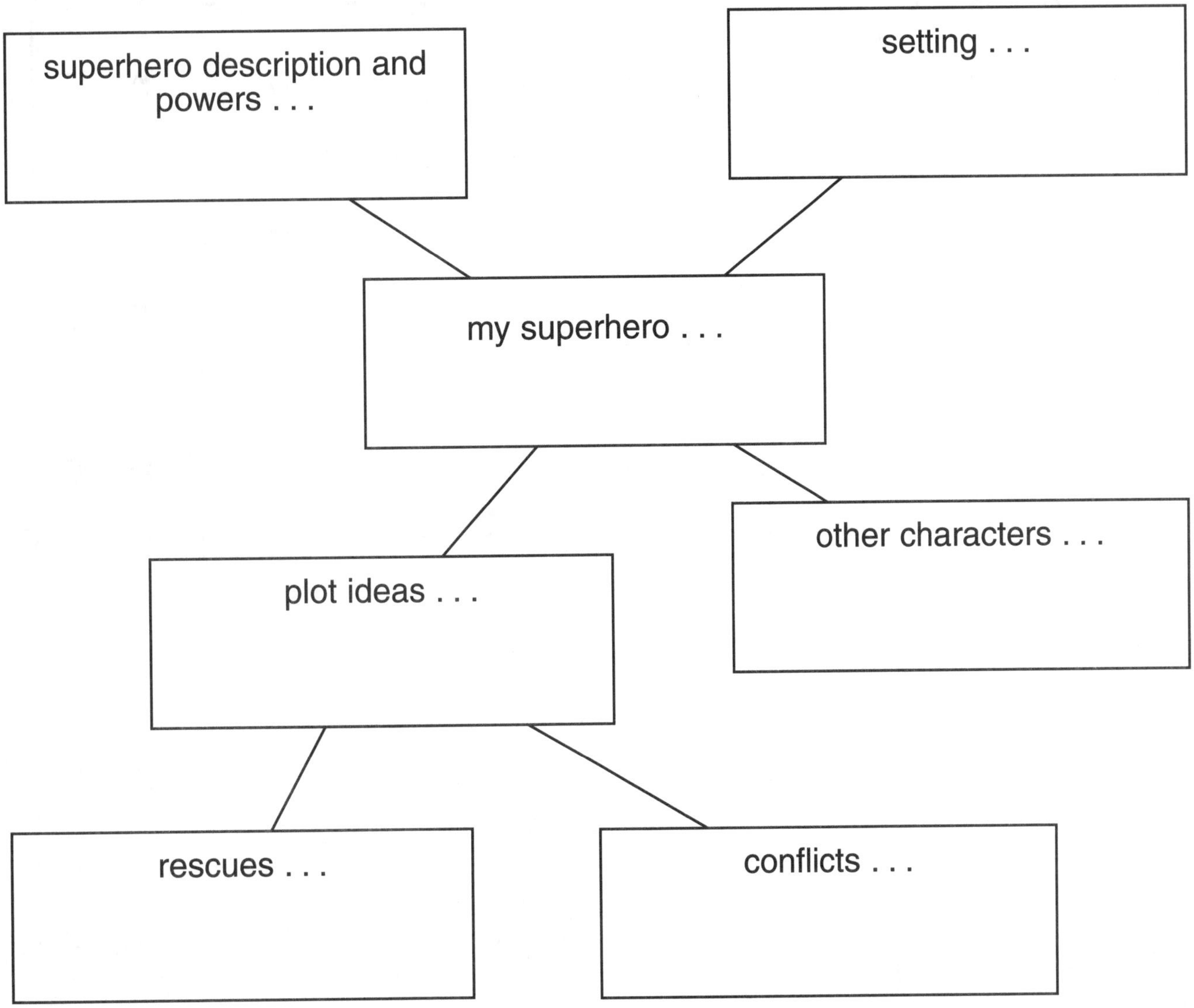

superhero description and powers . . .

setting . . .

my superhero . . .

other characters . . .

plot ideas . . .

rescues . . .

conflicts . . .

Adventures in Literature and Film

Find the names of these fictional and non-fictional characters who are known for their adventuresome experiences.

Alice in Wonderland, Aladdin, Robinson Crusoe, Swiss Family Robinson, Superman, Sherlock Holmes, Count of Monte Cristo, Three Musketeers, Hercules, Indiana Jones, Odysseus, Capt. Picard, Batman, Robin, Pecos Bill, Pocahantas, Tarzan, Lassie

S	U	P	E	R	M	A	N	I	N	D	I	A	N	A	J
H	E	R	C	U	L	E	S	C	E	I	S	S	A	L	O
E	A	S	E	M	U	S	K	E	T	E	E	R	S	X	N
R	B	W	E	S	U	P	R	A	M	E	N	D	V	A	E
L	E	I	R	D	P	O	C	A	H	O	N	T	A	S	S
O	G	S	H	F	H	L	J	U	B	A	T	M	A	N	L
C	I	S	T	A	R	Z	A	N	L	S	O	C	E	P	Z
K	K	F	A	M	I	L	Y	R	O	B	I	N	S	O	N
N	H	O	L	M	E	S	E	B	W	I	A	O	Y	D	C
I	P	I	C	A	R	D	R	P	C	L	H	T	M	Y	R
D	T	M	Q	S	N	T	O	F	M	L	F	M	J	S	U
D	P	T	N	O	O	N	B	D	O	O	N	A	O	S	S
A	A	R	W	E	Q	U	I	K	N	I	N	N	G	E	O
L	C	N	R	P	L	O	N	C	R	I	S	T	O	U	E
A	L	I	C	E	V	C	T	S	E	C	R	I	E	S	O

My Imaginary Great Adventure

REDI* In the film, *Bill and Ted's Excellent Adventure*, Bill and Ted go back in history to bring back the composer Beethoven, the U.S. President Lincoln, and the philosopher Socrates for a living history report. Now it is your turn to go back in time. Select one of the following people who were real-life adventurers in the field of medicine, science, sports, music, art, literature, human rights, and exploration. Bring him or her to class for your own living history report.

For you to do:

First: Select one of the adventurers from the list below.

Second: Read about your person and write a biography page containing as much information as you can find.

Third: Make a miniature model of your person using cardboard for the body, fabric for clothing, and yarn for hair. Cut out facial features from magazines or draw them yourself.

- John Glenn
- Jacques Cousteau
- Jackie Robinson
- Babe Didrickson
- Christian Barnard
- Madame Curie
- Joseph Lister
- Florence Nightingale
- Louis Pasteur
- Raul Wallenberg
- Albert Sweitzer
- Stanley Livingston
- Edmund Hillary
- Neil Armstrong
- Janet Guthrie
- Meriwether Lewis
- William Clark
- Ferdinand Magellan
- Marco Polo
- Cesar Chavez
- Marian Anderson
- Wolfgang Amadeus Mozart
- Albert Einstein
- Michelangelo
- Leonardo da Vinci
- William Shakespeare
- Rosa Parks
- Martin Luther King, Jr.
- Benjamin Franklin
- Harriet Tubman
- Sitting Bull
- Albert Sabin
- Sandra Day O'Connor
- Dwight D. Eisenhower
- Joan of Arc
- Martin Luther
- Christopher Columbus
- George Washington
- Yuri Gagarin
- Indira Ghandi

**Research-Explore-Discover-Investigate*

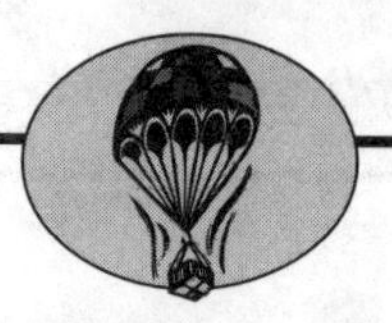

Getting to Know You

REDI* Get to know some of history's most interesting people. As you find each person in an encyclopedia, biography book, or other source, fill in the discovery chart.

Name	Occupation	Years Lived	Accomplishment
1. John Glenn			
2. Jacques Cousteau			
3. Jackie Robinson			
4. Babe Didrickson			
5. Christian Barnard			
6. Madame Curie			
7. Joseph Lister			
8. Florence Nightingale			
9. Louis Pasteur			
10. Raul Wallenberg			
11. Albert Sweitzer			
12. Stanley Livingston			
13. Edmund Hillary			
14. Neil Armstrong			
15. Janet Guthrie			
16. Meriwether Lewis			
17. William Clark			
18. Ferdinand Magellan			
19. Marco Polo			
20. Cesar Chavez			
21. Marian Anderson			
22. Wolfgang Amadeus Mozart			
23. Albert Einstein			
24. Michelangelo			
25. Leonardo da Vinci			
26. William Shakespeare			
27. Rosa Parks			
28. Martin Luther King, Jr.			
29. Benjamin Franklin			
30. Harriet Tubman			
31. Sitting Bull			
32. Albert Sabin			
33. Sandra Day O'Connor			
34. Dwight D. Eisenhower			
35. Joan of Arc			
36. Martin Luther			
37. Christopher Columbus			
38. George Washington			
39. Yuri Gagarin			
40. Indira Ghandi			

**Research-Explore-Discover-Investigate*

Pets and Friends

Teacher Spin-Off Page

Pre-Writing Discussion Ideas

1. Ask how people become best friends. What qualities are important in a best friend?
2. Take a class survey and find out how many students have pets. Draw boxes on the chalkboard for categories (large pets, small pets, water pets, etc.).
3. Talk about how people name their pets. Are names always an indicator of the pet's reputation? Would you name your Doberman "Fifi" or your Chihuahua "Spike"? Discuss.
4. Ask if students have seen any unusual pet tricks on television.
5. Discuss "pet" films and novels such as *Homeward Bound, Shiloh, Old Yeller, The Aristocats, 101 Dalmatians, Beethoven, Benji, Where the Red Fern Grows, The Voyages of Dr. Doolittle, James Herriot's All Creatures Great and Small,* and *Animal Stories.* Also for good reading and discussion, read excerpts of *The Compassion of Animals, True Stories of Animal Courage and Kindness* by K. Kreisler, and *Chicken Soup for the Pet Lover's Soul.*
6. Discuss presidential pets such as President Lincoln's dog, Fido, or Franklin Roosevelt's Fala. Lyndon Johnson's beagles, Him and Her, were the focus of a controversy with animal rights activists when President Johnson was photographed picking up Him by the ears. President Bush's Millie had puppies in the White House and also "wrote" a book. Talk about the First Cat, Socks.
7. Talk about security and protection dogs and the reputation they have (Rottweilers, Dobermans, Pit Bulls, German Shepherds). What kind of training should these dogs have? Are they born with certain instincts that other dogs do not have? Are they more trainable than other dogs?

Word Bank Activities

1. Go over the word bank and have students say the words orally.
2. Discuss the animals' names and have students guess the countries in which the animals originated. For example, "bichon frise" is French—*bichon*=lapdog + *frise*=curly. So a bichon frise is a curly lapdog.
3. Have students do a name study for the following animal names: Pekingese, rottweiler, Chihuahuas, Abyssinian, Siamese, Pomeranian, Lhasa apso, keeshond, Dalmatian, akita, Shar-Pei, dachsund, Weimeraner, Corgi, schipperkes, Persian.
4. Make a list of idioms and idiomatic expressions after talking about "it's raining cats and dogs."

In the Writing Workshop

1. Write the following addresses on the board so that the students can consider writing a personal letter regarding support for animal rights. Students may also write requesting information regarding animal care and protection.

Society for the Prevention of Cruelty to Animals (SPCA)
(Consult the Yellow Pages to find your local chapter.)

People for the Ethical Treatment of Animals
501 Front Street
Norfolk, Virginia 23510

Greenpeace
1611 Connecticut Avenue, N.W.
Washington DC 20016

Doris Day Animal League
227 Massachusetts Avenue, N.E.
Washington DC 20002

Teacher Spin-Off Page *(cont.)*

In the Writing Workshop *(cont.)*

2. Many animal protection organizations sponsor essay and poster-making contests. Contact these agencies for information so that your students may participate.
3. Have students write concrete animal poems (in the shape of the animal) and create a bulletin board of animal poetry.
4. Make an anthology of animal stories by having each student write an animal anecdote. Make copies for circulation among the students.

Say It Without Words

1. Make individual collages of animal pictures collected from magazines. Students might want to include their own pet pictures, also.
2. For a fun project, have students make a video of their pet and show it to the class.
3. Set up a classroom aquarium and have students monitor the conditions daily.
4. Play animal charades and animal Pictionary.

Analytical Lifeskill

1. Contact the SPCA (Society for the Prevention of Cruelty to Animals) and schedule a special speaker for your class. The SPCA has a variety of educational programs that can be presented to students.
2. Contact your local television stations to find out if they are sponsoring any special animal-awareness programs during the year. Invite someone from the station to talk.
3. Schedule a visit to a veterinarian or have a veterinarian visit your class.
4. Invite the police K-9 unit officer to speak to your class to talk about a police dog's job.
5. Make your students aware of visitation programs in rest homes, rehabilitation centers, and other care facilities in which pets are used in healing and therapy.
6. Obtain information about training for guide dogs for the blind.
7. Find out more about "assistance" dogs who act as the "arms and legs" of people who are disabled.

Answer Key

Page 85 1. h 2. f 3. v 4. j 5. i 6. y 7. g 8. n 9. w 10. l 11. m 12. k 13. x 14. o 15. e 16. d 17. c 18. u 19. b 20. q 21. p 22. t 23. s 24. a 25. r

Page 86 1. 3,456 in^3; 14.96 gal; 124.18 lbs 2. 19,200 in^3; 83.12 gal; 689.87 lbs 3. 10,240 in^3; 44.33 gal; 367.93 lbs 4. 24,000 in^3; 103.9 gal; 862.34 lbs 5. 300,000 in^3; 1,298.7 gal; 10,779.22 lbs

Page 87 Kittycat

Page 89 1. f 2. g 3. a 4. b 5. e 6. c 7. d 8. h

Page 97 1. Old Dan and Little Ann 2. Black Beauty 3. the wolf dog 4. Rascal the raccoon 5. Old Yeller 6. Wishbone 7. Ren and Stimpy 8. Garfield and lasagna 9. Dino and Fred 10. Cujo the bad dog 11. Astro and the Jetsons 12. pet rock 13. chia pet 14. B-I-N-G-O and the farmer 15. Beethoven the St. Bernard 16. Barkley and Big Bird 17. Toto and Dorothy 18. Lassie and Timmy 19. Dogbert and Dilbert 20. Snoopy and Charlie Brown 21. Shadow and Peter

Word Bank

For some people, having a dog, cat or goldfish is enough to satisfy the need for a pet. On the other hand, others enjoy the company of more unusual creatures.

Question: Which of the word bank words could be considered good pets?

For you to do: Mark the dog words with a "D" and the cat words with a "C". What other types of pets can you identify?

1. bichon frise
2. Pekingese
3. hamster
4. veterinarian
5. rottweiler
6. guinea pig
7. iguana
8. canine
9. rabies
10. chimpanzee
11. retriever
12. Doberman pinscher
13. Chihuahua
14. Chesire
15. tortoise
16. Abyssinian
17. Siamese
18. Pomeranian
19. Lhasa apso
20. spaniel
21. keeshond

22. Dalmatian
23. Akita
24. boa constrictor
25. rodents
26. Shar-Pei
27. dachshund
28. Weimaraner
29. malamute
30. corgi
31. schipperkes
32. Himalayan
33. Angora
34. Manx
35. Persian
36. calico
37. tabby
38. feline
39. grayhound
40. quarterhorse
41. Appaloosa
42. palomino

It's Raining Cats and Dogs

Wordbank Activity

Our everyday conversation is sprinkled with dog and cat references. How many of these dog and cat words and phrases do you know? Quiz yourself by matching the word or phrase with its meaning.

1. ______ dog-tired
2. ______ dogwood
3. ______ dog paddle
4. ______ dog days
5. ______ hot dog
6. ______ Dogbert
7. ______ dog tag
8. ______ dog eared
9. ______ doggy bag
10. ______ dog star
11. ______ prairie dog
12. ______ dog and pony show
13. ______ dog run
14. ______ underdog
15. ______ cat's cradle
16. ______ cat's meow
17. ______ cat scan
18. ______ catnap
19. ______ catnip
20. ______ catfish
21. ______ catsup
22. ______ CATS
23. ______ catacomb
24. ______ catapult
25. ______ catalogue

a. launching mechanism
b. herb
c. computerized axial tomography
d. one of the best
e. string game
f. flowering tree
g. metal I.D.
h. worn out
i. roast it on a stick
j. hot weather
k. big production
l. Sirius
m. rodent
n. wrinkled pages
o. not expected to win
p. ketchup
q. short barbs
r. publication of goods
s. underground tunnels and chambers
t. Andrew Lloyd Weber musical
u. snooze
v. swimming stroke
w. for leftovers
x. enclosed exercise pen
y. cartoon character

For further thought What kind of picture do you see when someone says, "It's raining cats and dogs"? If you were a meteorologist, what weather information would you be giving your viewers if you used this idiomatic expression?

Aquarium Weights and Measurements

Aquariums come in many shapes and sizes. Imagine that you are setting up an aquarium in your house and need to know how many gallons of water your aquarium will hold and how heavy your water-filled aquarium will be. Here is a formula to help you figure these weights and measurements.

Formula: Length x Width x Height = Volume (how much space there is within the aquarium in cubic inches)

Sample: Your aquarium is 12" x 12" x 20"

The volume is: ____2880____ cubic inches

Now divide the volume by 231 cubic inches to determine the number of gallons of water you will need to fill your aquarium.

The number of gallons of water needed to fill: ____12.47 gallons____

Then multiply the number of gallons by 8.3 pounds (this is how much one gallon of water weighs) to see how heavy your aquarium will be with water in it.

The weight of my aquarium is ____103.48____ pounds

Using the formula, find the missing information for the following aquariums: (Round answers to the nearest hundredth)

1. 24" x 12" x 12" How many cubic inches? ________________
   How many gallons of water? ________________
   How heavy (in pounds)? ________________
2. 48" x 20" x 20" How many cubic inches? ________________
   How many gallons of water? ________________
   How heavy (in pounds)? ________________
3. 40" x 16" x 16" How many cubic inches? ________________
   How many gallons of water? ________________
   How heavy (in pounds)? ________________
4. 60" x 20" x 20" How many cubic inches? ________________
   How many gallons of water? ________________
   How heavy (in pounds)? ________________
5. 120" x 50" x 50" How many cubic inches? ________________
   How many gallons of water? ________________
   How heavy (in pounds)? ________________

For further thought: In what situations would it be important to know the weight of your water-filled aquarium?

Aquarium Fish Find

The names of the fish marked with asterisks (*) are hidden in the puzzle below. Can you find them? Some words may be used twice and some words are connected to other words.

*stickleback	*shark catfish	*anemone fish	*angelfish	*gobies
*clowns	*rainbows	*mudskippers	*dottybacks	*blennies
*butterfly fish	*darters	four-eyed fish	plecostomus	chichlids
*goldfish	mollies	*gouramis	*damsels	*danios
electric fish	*spiny eels	yellow tang	cardinal fish	archer fish
*puffers	*rasboras	*seahorse	Siamese fighter (beta)	

Unscramble the bold-faced letters to learn what you should keep out of the aquarium.

S	P	I	N	Y	E	E	L	S	G	J	R	**K**	N	C	D
H	T	G	O	U	R	A	M	I	S	U	H	M	P	A	A
A	N	**I**	F	L	Y	O	G	O	B	I	E	S	R	D	M
R	R	A	C	E	P	S	O	D	V	O	A	T	V	Y	S
K	A	M	Z	K	Q	Q	L	M	I	K	E	J	K	L	E
C	I	R	X	I	L	W	D	**T**	X	R	I	W	M	B	L
A	N	E	M	O	N	E	F	I	S	H	K	Q	Y	X	S
T	B	S	U	G	M	E	B	U	T	T	E	R	F	L	Y
F	O	R	D	O	T	T	Y	A	N	G	E	L	I	O	F
I	W	E	S	P	Z	U	B	**Y**	C	X	U	I	S	V	I
S	S	F	K	S	H	N	A	H	L	K	G	D	H	D	S
H	Q	F	I	F	R	E	**C**	S	O	E	W	Z	C	Z	H
Q	C	U	P	J	F	T	K	B	W	E	S	L	B	U	E
A	B	P	P	B	O	V	S	D	N	S	O	I	N	A	D
L	F	N	E	T	W	G	R	A	S	B	O	R	A	S	C
R	H	**T**	R	B	L	E	N	N	I	E	S	G	F	J	H
C	J	P	S	E	A	H	O	R	S	E	A	C	I	K	**A**

Something Fishy Art Project

In this project you will be given supplies to design and create your own aquarium. Fill your aquarium with fish and aquatic plants. Your fish can be real (see some of the varieties listed on page 87) or you can create your own varieties. Use your imagination and enjoy making your underwater fish world.

Materials: one large piece of construction paper, several smaller pieces of construction paper in various colors, art tissue paper (wad into small pieces and glue onto the fish design for a mosaic effect), pieces of aluminum wrap for neon glow-in-the-dark fish, glitter, glue/glue stick

For further thought:

1. Have you ever had a fish for a pet?
2. Would you enjoy having an aquarium and fish for pets?
3. What are some of the advantages of having a fish for a pet?
   a. ____________________
   b. ____________________
   c. ____________________
   d. ____________________
4. What are some of the disadvantages of having a fish for a pet?
   a. ____________________
   b. ____________________
   c. ____________________
   d. ____________________

For you to do:

Look in the dictionary to find out what these words mean.

1. ceviche ____________________
2. bouillabaisse____________________
3. salinity ____________________
4. filtration ____________________

Petite Pets

Sometimes aquarium-type habitats are used for pets such as hamsters, guinea pigs, mice, rats, snakes, lizards, iguanas, and chameleons. Match the names and descriptions to see how much you know about these small pets.

________	1. hamster	a. can change colors depending on its moods and environment
________	2. iguana	b. short-eared domesticated rodent
________	3. chameleon	c. deaf, limbless reptile
________	4. guinea pig	d. rounded ears and pointed nose (or snout)
________	5. rat	e. long-tailed rodent
________	6. snake	f. cheek pouches for food storage
________	7. mouse	g. spiny back/often too large to be a pet
________	8. lizard	h. can be 3 inches to 10 feet long (Komodo)

Think about this:

Many movies have been made about huge reptiles that slither out of swampbeds at night to scare everyone. After all, Godzilla is just a really large lizard! But what would happen if your cute two-inch tall hamster suddenly grew to be ten feet tall! Where would it sleep? What would it eat? Would it still be friendly or would it undergo a personality transformation and become dangerous?

For you to do:

Write a story about one of the "petite pets" listed above. Use the story preparation boxes to get started. Draw a "before" and "after" picture of your pet.

Your pet before the big change	**Your pet after the change**
What caused the transformation?	**What problems have been created?**
Can your pet be returned to its original state?	**What is the future for your pet?**

My Best Pet

Today's Reflection: The 1950s television program *Lassie,* based on the novel *Lassie, Come Home* by Eric Knight, featured a beautiful collie. Lassie exhibited all of the best character traits in a pet. She was loyal, brave, fun, loving, helpful, and very smart. Lassie lived in the country with her owner Timmy, and Timmy's parents. Each episode featured Lassie running through the fields in an exciting story of rescue, heroism, and adventure.

Not everyone can have a pet such as Lassie, though. People who live in the city may enjoy smaller pets, such as cats, reptiles, birds, hamsters, fish, or even snakes. There are all kinds of pets to fit the needs of all kinds of people.

For you to do: Answer the following questions as you prepare to write today's reflection:

1. What kinds of pets have you had?____________________
2. What has been your favorite pet? ____________________
3. What kinds of things did you do to take care of your pet?____________________
4. Tell an anecdote (short story) about your pet. This could be something serious or funny.

   ____

   ____
5. If you don't have a pet, write about a pet that you would like to have or write about someone else's pet that you know.

   ____

   ____

Just for Fun:

Make up alliterative names for each of the following animals using the example as a model.

Example: Marvin the marvelous Malamute (the repeated "m" sound makes this an alliterative phrase). Now it's your turn.

1. Pekingese ____________________
2. rottweiler ____________________
3. iguana____________________
4. tortoise ____________________
5. Dalmatian____________________
6. boa ____________________
7. Weimaraner ____________________
8. tabby____________________
9. dachshund ____________________
10. Appaloosa ____________________

Respect All Creatures Great and Small

Today's Reflection: Some people treat their pets as if they were their own children . . . they spoil, pamper, indulge, and really love their pets. They are good to these animals that have been entrusted to their care. Other people ignore their pets, or even worse, neglect them and/or abuse them. Think about the following questions as you prepare to write today's reflection.

1. Do animals have feelings? ____________________
2. If you answered "yes," what kinds of feelings do you think they have? ____________________
3. Can animals be happy or sad? ____________________
4. Do animals have rights in the same way that people have rights? ____________________
5. What makes animals different from people? ____________________

For further thought:

Animals (particularly beagles, guinea pigs, and rabbits) have always been used for medical experimentation. In recent years animals have also been used for cosmetic experimentation. Most of these animals die or are "put to sleep" (euthanized) when they have fulfilled their usefulness to the laboratory.

For you to do: Write a reflection expressing your thoughts about the use of animals for experimentation.

Note: This is not a simple issue. Surgical procedures, drug research, and other medical treatments are made possible on humans because of the testing that has been done on animals. Consider both sides of the issue as you write your reflection.

Brainstorm your thoughts here.

Pro (reasons in favor of animal use)	Con (reasons against animal use)

My Pet Peeves

A pet peeve is something that really "gets to you," something that is really irritating. For some people, leaving the cap off the toothpaste is a pet peeve. Think about your pet peeves and write them below. Then brainstorm possible solutions that will help rid you of your pet peeves or at least help you live with them.

Use complete sentences and begin with phrases such as "I really get annoyed when . . ." or "I really dislike it when . . ." or "A pet peeve I have is . . . ."

My Pet Peeves

1. ____
2. ____
3. ____
4. ____
5. ____
6. ____
7. ____
8. ____
9. ____
10. ____
11. ____
12. ____

Possible Solutions

For further thought: Analyze the expression "pet peeve" and think about why the word "pet" is used.

Amazing Animal Facts Scavenger Hunt

REDI* Do some detective work and go on a library scavenger hunt to find the answers to the following questions.

Find the answer to the following questions:

1. What is the American Kennel Club? ____________________
2. What does it mean if a dog is "registered"? ____________________
3. What animal did the United States of America use to test space travel? ____________________
4. Name the dog that President and Mrs. Bush brought to the White House. ____________________
5. What is the name of Chelsea Clinton's cat? ____________________
6. Why are Pavlov's dogs so famous in the world of behavioral studies? ____________________
7. Why is the Animal Welfare Act of 1990 important for animals? ____________________
8. Why are animal rights activists opposed to vivisection? ____________________
9. When was the American Humane Society established? ____________________
10. What are the primary objectives of this organization? ____________________
11. When was the organization "People for the Ethical Treatment of Animals" established?

    ____
12. What are the primary objectives of this organization? ____________________
13. When was the Society for the Prevention of Cruelty to Animals (SPCA) established?

    ____
14. What are the primary objectives of this organization? ____________________
15. Where is the nearest SPCA in your area? ____________________
16. What kinds of services are offered to animals and animal owners? ____________________
17. Why did President Lyndon Johnson upset many animal owners in his treatment of his beagle "Him"?

    ____
18. Locate information about Tabitha, the cat who accidentally flew 30,000 miles in 12 days. Where did she go?

    ____
19. What is the "pet rock" and what does it do? ____________________
20. What is the origin of the "Chia Pet" and what does it do? ____________________

* *Research-Explore-Discover-Investigate*

Comics and Cartooning

Do you read the comic pages in the newspaper? Do you know someone who does? Do you have a favorite comic strip character or cartoon character? Comic strips became popular in American newspapers in the late 1800s. People looked forward to reading their favorite comic strip and newspaper sales increased! Most newspapers today have at least one full page of comics, and people still have their favorites. Comic strips can also be found in magazines, books, and inside the wrapping of Bazooka Bubble Gum.

Some of these early comic strip characters became so famous that movies, musicals, and toys were made based on the characters. How many of these comic strips are familiar to you?

From the early days of comic strips:

- Dick Tracy
- Buck Rogers
- Tarzan
- Flash Gordon
- Li'l Abner
- Little Orphan Annie

Which modern-day comic strips can you name? ______________________________

____

____

____

Now It's Your Turn!

1. Create a comic strip character (person or animal).
2. Write a narrative (what the character will say).
3. Decide on a title for your comic strip.
4. Divide your paper into six panels or boxes and create your comic strip in the boxes.
5. Color your work.

For Further Fun:

1. Take a poll and ask your classmates, family members, and friends which comic strip they enjoy the most.
2. Bring in newspaper clippings of comic strips you enjoy.

Animal Rights

Let's Talk About It: Our pets can't use words to communicate their needs so we need to understand their language. Animals communicate with sounds and body language. If your pet isn't feeling well, he or she may just lie around a lot instead of chasing the birds or his or her favorite ball. But if animals could talk about their needs, what would they tell us?

For you to do: Create a 10-point Animal Bill of Rights document that tells us how to take care of animals and meet their needs. As you write, put yourself in their "paws" and think through every possible situation that animals encounter.

Example: *All animals have the right to fresh water.*

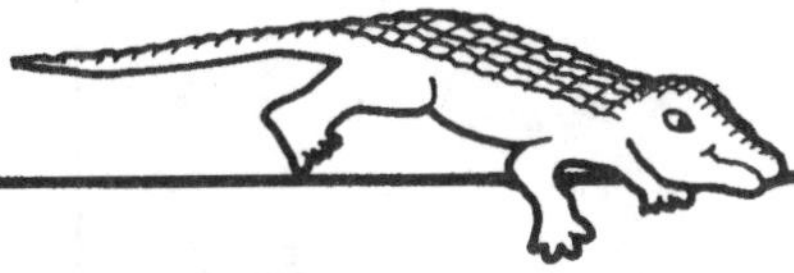

The Animal Bill of Rights

1. ______________________________
2. ______________________________
3. ______________________________
4. ______________________________ 
5. ______________________________
6. ______________________________
7. ______________________________
8. ______________________________
9. ______________________________
10. ______________________________

Art Activity

Make a poster for your Animal Bill of Rights and illustrate it. Experiment with different handwriting styles and try to make the poster look like a historical document.

Busy Career Dogs

REDI* Not all dogs get to spend their days sleeping in the shade or lying next to the fireplace. While many dogs call it a day's work after they have brought in the morning newspaper, other dogs work a full day doing very important tasks. Research the following categories and record any information you find.

Assistance Dogs for the Handicapped	Visiting Dogs for the sick and elderly
Show Dogs/Travel Dogs	**Guide Dogs for the Blind**
Herding Dogs	**Law Enforcement Dogs**

* *Research-Explore-Discover-Investigate*

Fictional Animal Friends

Just for Fun: These animal characters came from the imaginations of writers and cartoonists. Match the name in column A to the name or word in column B that completes each phrase.

Column A	Column B
1. Old Dan ______	and the farmer
2. Black ______	the wolf dog
3. Kavik ______	and lasagna
4. Rascal ______	and Stimpy
5. Old ______	and Timmy
6. Wish ______	and Dilbert
7. Ren ______	Beauty
8. Garfield ______	and Little Ann
9. Dino ______	the racoon
10. Cujo ______	and Dorothy
11. Astro ______	and Charlie Brown
12. pet ______	the bad dog
13. Chia ______	and the Jetsons
14. B-I-N-G-O ______	Yeller
15. Beethoven ______	bone
16. Barkley ______	the St. Bernard
17. Toto ______	and Big Bird
18. Lassie ______	and Peter
19. Dogbert ______	rock
20. Snoopy ______	pet
21. Shadow ______	and Fred

Other fictional animals that you can name:

______

______

______

______

______

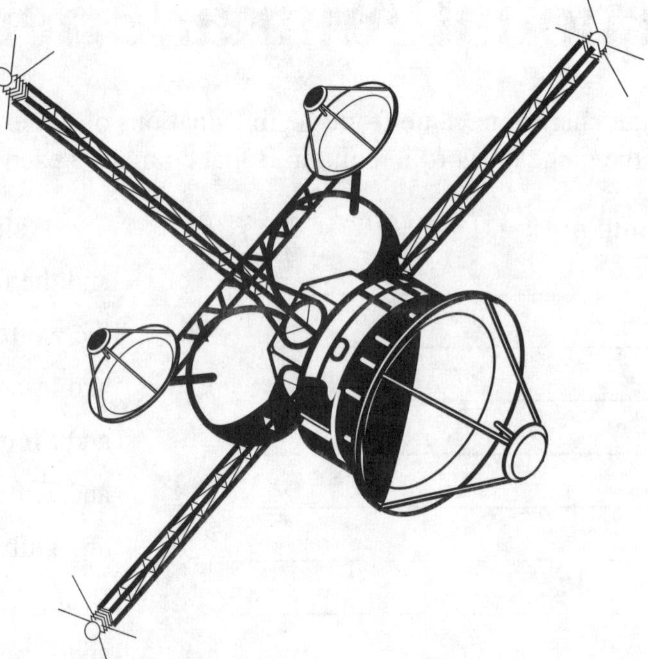

Communication and Connections

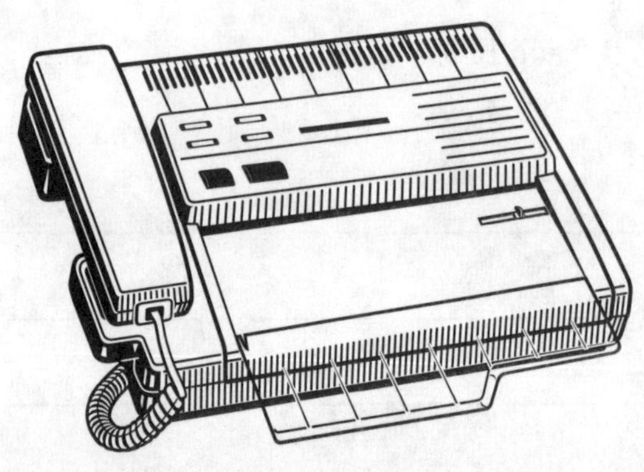

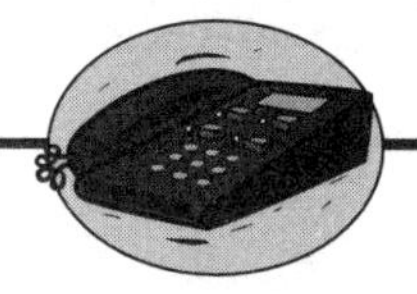

Spin-Off Teacher Page

Pre-Writing Discussion Ideas

1. "Who was the first person with whom you talked today?" Ask this question to your students to begin a discussion of communication exchanges. Ask what kinds of written communication they have read or heard (school announcements, newspaper, radio, etc.)
2. Develop student awareness by giving them pre-cut construction paper telephones. Have students write down their phone's special features (call-waiting, answering machine, more than one phone line, on-line electronic mail, etc.) on their paper telephones.
3. Discuss a baby's "pre-language" sounds and body language. Ask "How does a baby tell you he's hungry? How does a baby tell you he doesn't feel well? Are you glad we grow out of this 'language' stage?"
4. Bring newspapers for students to study. Have them take notice of the different sections and organization of the paper. Ask students which portion of the newspaper would they most enjoy putting together.
5. Talk about different forms of communication in the classroom (chalkboard, whiteboard, overhead, intercom, telephone, computer, handouts, verbal, notes, textbooks etc.) Have a student "recorder" or "scribe" write these on the board.
6. Talk about the "old days" when phone lines were party lines and you had to wait for the other person to get off the phone before you could make your call.
7. Bring in a rotary-dial telephone and talk about the limited features.
8. Discuss the fading art of letter-writing.
9. Have students discuss "poor communication" with parents, teachers, their peers. What causes poor communication or a breakdown of communication?
10. Have students discuss what things have to happen in order to have good communication.
11. Discuss "mass media" and the importance of keeping people informed.
12. Think about what would happen if we couldn't get weather reports.
13. What other information do we get from mass media sources that give health and safety information? (e-coli outbreak, hurricane warnings, etc.)
14. Invite a speaker from "Toastmasters" or another civic group to give students public speaking tips.
15. Find out which students speak another language fluently and have them tell how they learned more than one language.

Word Bank Activities

1. Introduce the word bank words and have students write related words. For example, "connection" can become "connected," "disconnect," or "disconnection."
2. Use the words "prefix," "suffix," "synonym" and "antonym" throughout the word bank.
3. Have the students determine which words in the word bank are nouns (review person, place, thing, idea).

Spin-Off Teacher Page *(cont.)*

4. Have students create their own word search using words from the Treasure Chest.

Possible Projects

1. Videotape a news broadcast and have students write only the "title" of each report. Then, in groups, have the students compile as much information as they remember on each report. Emphasize how organized and clear communication helps the listener retain more information.
2. Form news teams and have the students videotape a news program.
3. Simulate a radio station with microphones and a tape recorder or CD player. Have a team of students create a radio program.
4. Have students create a classroom newspaper. Let students volunteer for positions (managing editor, publisher, layout, graphics, proofreader, sports reporter, activities reporter, social reporter, world news, local news, etc.). Have students be responsible for all aspects except printing.
5. Invite a local newspaper reporter to come to class to talk about his or her job.
6. Find out if your local newspapers offer free classroom subscriptions or get a sponsor to provide a weekly or daily newspaper for your students. Have a recycling system in place for your papers.

In the Writing Workshop

1. Have students select one person from the "Great Negotiators and Communicators" list or randomly distribute 3" x 5" (8 cm x 13 cm) cards that already have a name supplied. Let students search for biographical information on the person which they have selected or been given and write a mini-biography (1/2–1 page) sketch.
2. Create a bulletin board with each mini-biography sketch posted on 1/2 sheet of poster board. Have students creatively write the name of their person on the poster board.
3. Have students write about how it would feel to live in a silent world. What would they miss hearing? Do this writing after a silent class period (see number two below).

Say It Without Words

1. Have each student learn to "say" his or her name using the signing alphabet.
2. For one class period, use no spoken words for communication. You and your students may use body language or notes but no oral communication.
3. Give students a "Say It Without Words" sheet for "free drawing" during the class period.

Analytical Lifeskill

1. Explain how "webbing" or "mapping" is a helpful pre-writing technique. Use the mass media topic as a class mapping activity on the board. Use categories such as journalism (newspapers, magazines), radio, and/or television.
2. Have students develop individual maps/webs on topics of their choice.
3. Let students share their maps/webs in groups to stimulate vocabulary development. Students can add to each other's maps/webs.

Spin-Off Teacher Page *(cont.)*

In the Library

1. As students go on the "Communication Treasure Hunt" encourage them to move out of the reference section of the library and into the book shelves. Point them to the communication section (radio, television, photography, journalism, telecommunications, etc.).
2. Encourage students to let their research lead them to other related topics which might be of interest to them.
3. Give students an "Extra, Extra, Read All About It" page on which they can log information they find on a topic of their own finding.

Answer Key

Page 110

1. a reading system for the blind
2. "The Queen's Messenger."
3. Federal Communication Commission
4. FM
5. AM
6. CB
7. science of communication by codes
8. birds
9. whales
10. languages
11. China
12. Johann Gutenberg
13. smoke, drums, horns
14. pigeons
15. Samuel Morse
16. fiberoptic cables
17. communication satellites
18. typewriters
19. microphone, megaphone
20. Thomas Gallaudet
21. American Sign Language
22. hearing aids
23. filibuster
24. free speech
25. to convey messages
26. beacon
27. fax
28. electronic mail
29. phonograph
30. compact disc
31. cryptographers
32. pictographs and hieroglyphs
33. telegrams
34. Mr. Bell and Mr. Watson
35. Thomas Edison
36. overhead projector, filmstrip projector
37. answering machine
38. journalists
39. radio, television, magazines, newspapers
40. antenna

Word Bank

1. transmission
2. contact
3. connection
4. letter
5. antenna
6. beacon
7. alphabet
8. airmail
9. Braille
10. phonograph
11. broadcasting
12. facsimile
13. citizen's band radio
14. compact disc
15. satellite communications
16. global positioning system
17. answering machine
18. cryptography
19. frequency
20. codes
21. languages
22. pictographic
23. hieroglyphics
24. typesetting machines
25. Morse code
26. electrical
27. wireless signals
28. teletype
29. telex
30. lithography
31. daguerreotype
32. kinetoscope
33. computer
34. laser
35. fiberoptic cable
36. negotiations
37. peace talks
38. arbitrator
39. arbitration
40. negotiator
41. record
42. telegraph
43. telephone
44. telecommunication
45. mass media
46. magazine
47. microphone
48. newspaper
49. amplification
50. headset
51. operator
52. cell phone
53. hearing impaired
54. closed captioned
55. visually impaired
56. slang
57. formal language
58. informal language
59. idiom
60. dialect
61. argumentation
62. persuasion
63. censorship
64. rebus
65. literacy
66. runes
67. shorthand
68. paleography
69. calligraphy
70. electronic mail
71. verbal communication
72. non-verbal communication
73. oral language
74. American Sign Language
75. transistor
76. walkie-talkie
77. intercom
78. cliche
79. cable
80. writing
81. speech

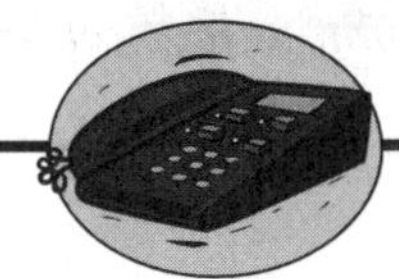

Communication Tools Word Search

The **brush**, **chalk**, **pointed stylus**, **quill**, **fountain pen**, **ballpoint pen**, and **pencil** are just some of the **writing implements** that people have used over the centuries. These writing implements, or tools, have been used on **paper** (which is made from **wood pulp**), **papyrus** (which comes from the stalk of the papyrus reeds), **parchment** (made from the untanned skins of sheep or goats), and **vellum** (which is parchment made from calf or lambskin). Even **silk** has been used as a writing surface on which to record communication from one person to another. Long ago a **mallet** and **chisel** were used to pound communication onto **stone tablets** and **walls**. Today, a popular writing implement is the **computer**. What kinds of **writing tools** do you think people will be using 100 years from now?

To do: Find the 20 words or terms in bold-faced type in the word search below. Letters may be used more than once.

P	A	P	Y	R	U	S	G	S	F	O	G	R	M	Y	L	T
O	E	B	M	A	L	L	E	T	O	Z	N	X	U	I	G	N
I	G	N	R	W	U	Q	S	O	U	A	I	E	L	E	R	E
N	B	K	C	H	A	L	K	N	N	X	S	I	L	R	D	M
T	R	L	U	I	O	T	E	E	T	A	N	L	E	T	S	H
E	U	V	E	Y	L	W	L	I	A	T	C	P	V	Q	S	C
D	S	T	Y	L	U	S	Y	J	I	G	A	F	K	X	L	R
H	H	I	T	X	M	K	L	K	N	P	E	N	P	U	O	A
J	R	S	Z	S	V	X	L	O	L	W	U	H	O	W	O	P
W	R	I	T	I	N	G	I	M	P	L	E	M	E	N	T	S
O	P	L	E	O	E	N	U	Q	W	R	I	T	I	N	G	H
O	M	K	B	R	C	P	Q	J	M	A	V	J	T	S	Z	K
D	B	D	N	E	P	T	N	I	O	P	L	L	A	B	C	R
P	U	L	P	R	C	Z	C	H	I	S	E	L	N	V	F	S
A	C	O	M	P	U	T	E	R	P	A	Y	M	S	B	J	A

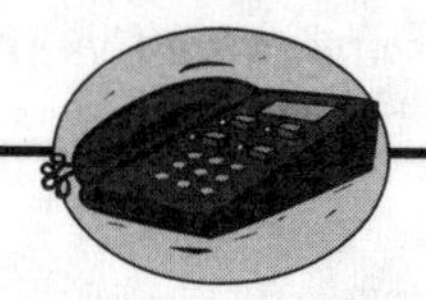

Great Negotiators

Have you ever been misunderstood? Have you ever felt that no one is listening to you? These problems are known as "communication breakdowns" and can cause a lot of difficulty at home, at school, and in the workplace. Sometimes when people or groups cannot communicate well, a third party is invited to "mediate," "arbitrate," or "negotiate." These mediators, arbitrators and negotiators are skilled listeners who are able to help repair the "communication breakdown" so that good communication can take place and conflicts can be solved. Read the following brief sketches about some of the world's greatest communicators who were able to bring about positive resolutions that affected many people.

Christopher Warren	In 1981 he negotiated the release of American hostages who were being held in Iran.
Jimmy Carter	A former U.S. president, he conducted peace negotiations between Israel and Egypt.
George Bush	As President of the U.S., he negotiated with Mikhail Gorbachev of the USSR to end the production of chemical weapons.
Frederick Willem DeKlerk	As president of South Africa, he negotiated a new constitution which gave political rights to the blacks of his country, ending apartheid.
Javier Perez de Cueller	A Peruvian diplomat and Secretary of the United Nations, he negotiated an end to the Iran/Iraq War in 1986; he also helped free the American hostages held in Lebanon.
Nelson Mandela	After his release from prison, he helped negotiate a new constitution for South Africa.
John Jay	An American statesman, he helped negotiate the Treaty of Paris which ended the American Revolution.
Henry Kissinger	A U.S. Secretary of State, his negotiations resulted in a cease-fire in the Vietnam War.
Dan Webster	He negotiated the boundary between the United States and Canada.
Cyrus Vance	This skilled negotiator served under two U.S. presidents and was at the Paris Peace Talks negotiating an end to the Vietnam War.
Jesse Jackson	An American clergyman and civil rights activist, he helped negotiate the release of Americans held hostage in Kuwait.
Menachim Begin	As Prime Minister of Israel, he negotiated the first peace treaty between Israel and the Arab world.

*An expert negotiator/mediator/arbitrator must be an excellent listener. Using complete sentences, list five qualities that a good listener must possess.

1. ____________________
2. ____________________
3. ____________________
4. ____________________
5. ____________________

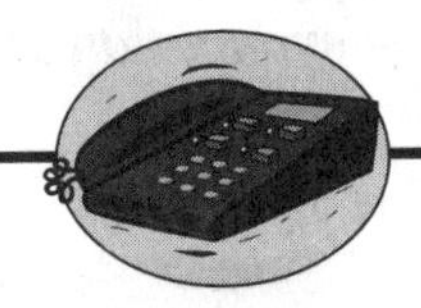

Great Communicators

Read about some of the world's greatest communicators who stood up for their beliefs and made a difference in history.

Vaclav Havel This former president of Czechoslovakia used his original plays to speak up for human rights issues.

Susan B. Anthony An excellent orator, she delivered speeches on behalf of women's rights.

Winston Churchill The former British Prime Minister, he gave speeches to his countrymen during World War II urging them to continue fighting and not give up.

Henry Ward Beecher An American clergyman, he preached against slavery.

Abraham Lincoln This U.S. President delivered the Gettysburg Address following a battle of the American Civil War.

Rachel Carson As an author and marine biologist, she raised public awareness of environmental issues through her writing.

Barbara Jordan While serving in the U.S. House of Representatives, she gave a speech in favor of impeaching President Richard Nixon.

Patrick Henry This patriot said, "Give me liberty or give me death," and helped lead the colonists to revolt against England.

Pearl Buck American writer whose work communicated understanding of China.

Jeanette Rankin First woman in the House of Representatives, she was an outspoken activist for peace.

Julia Ward Howe She composed "The Battle Hymn of the Republic," which rallied anti-slavery support during the American Civil War.

Sojourner Truth An American abolitionist, she was known for her preaching against slavery and for the rights of women.

Excellent communicators are found in all walks of life. Make a list of the top ten jobs that require the best communication skills and explain why these jobs demand people who can communicate well.

1. ______________________________
____
2. ______________________________
____
3. ______________________________
____
4. ______________________________
____
5. ______________________________
____
6. ______________________________
____
7. ______________________________
____
8. ______________________________
____
9. ______________________________
____
10. ______________________________
____

Organizing Information

Think About This: Alphabetizing is a skill that we call upon in our daily lives. What would happen in offices if files and information were randomly filed? Imagine your school office trying to find your transcripts or grade reports amid a mountain of unorganized, unalphabetized stacks. Information would be difficult or impossible to find. Alphabetizing provides a way to organize information for easy retrieval.

Your Task:

1. Combine the great negotiators and great communicators lists to create one alphabetized list. Alphabetize by last names.
2. Take your alphabetized list to the library and locate the following information for each person:
   a. date of birth
   b. place of birth
   c. number of years this person lived (lifespan) *Example:* (1906–1985)

Alphabetized Listing

Name:	Date of Birth	Place of Birth	Lifespan
1.			
2.			
3.			
4.			
5.			
6.			
7.			
8.			
9.			
10.			
11.			
12.			
13.			
14.			
15.			
16.			
17.			
18.			
19.			
20.			
21.			
22.			
23.			
24.			

Telling It Like It Is!

Today's Reflection: In our country, we are able to communicate freely because of our First Amendment, which guarantees freedom of speech. We are free to communicate our ideas and beliefs without censorship or fear of reprisal. Imagine that you are writing for a newspaper and you are trying to persuade your readership to adopt your point of view. Select one of the following topics and write an opinion page taking either side of the issue.

1. A longer school day or a shorter school day
2. Higher pay for emergency workers or higher pay for professional athletes
3. A four-day work week or a five-day work week
4. Legalizing drugs or not legalizing drugs
5. A higher minimum age for a driver's license or a lower minimum age
6. Mandatory "drunk driver" car sticker for those convicted of DUI (driving under the influence) or no sticker
7. Keeping the death penalty or eliminating the death penalty
8. Experimenting on animals only for medical research or for cosmetic research as well
9. Prosecuting juveniles who commit serious crimes as adults or prosecuting them as juveniles
10. National healthcare or private healthcare

Handy Tip of the Day: *Antonyms are words that have opposite meanings such as "freedom of speech" and "censorship." Synonyms are words that share the same meaning. Find other antonyms and synonyms for the words "freedom" and "censorship."*

Non-Verbal Signaling Devices

Non-verbal (without words) signaling devices are all around us. They are constantly guiding and directing our actions. These devices fall into two categories: safety and recreation. In the list below, tell what each signaling device is communicating.

Example:

buoy: it lets boats and ships know they are in dangerous water or they are entering a harbor

1. foghorn ____________________
2. microwave timer ____________________
3. lighthouse beacon ____________________
4. traffic signal ____________________
5. stop sign ____________________
6. broken white line on street ____________________
7. botts dots ____________________
8. double yellow line on street ____________________
9. automobile fuel gauge ____________________
10. pager/beeper ____________________
11. smoke alarm ____________________
12. sensor light ____________________
13. fire alarm ____________________
14. siren ____________________
15. watch dog ____________________
16. alarm clock ____________________
17. doorbell ____________________
18. clock face ____________________
19. plane runway lighting ____________________
20. bicycle reflectors ____________________
21. church bells ____________________
22. referee signals ____________________
23. base coach hand signals ____________________
24. football flags ____________________
25. school bell ____________________
26. "chirping bird" at pedestrian crossings ____________________
27. door knocker ____________________
28. emergency vehicle flashing lights ____________________

For further thought:
Can you think of some other non-verbal signaling devices and the messages they communicate?

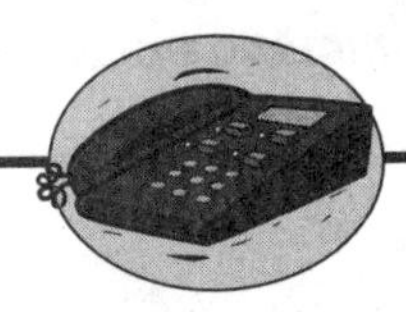

Making a Brochure

Communication is conveyed through sight and sound, but many people live in a world in which they cannot see or hear. How is communication then possible? Many people have given their lives to the task of making communication possible for those who are blind or deaf. Select a topic from the list below and make a brochure that includes information you have found. Use your own words and include illustrations.

- Charles Barbier
- Perkins School for the Blind
- Helen Keller
- Anne Sullivan
- Florida School for the Blind
- Stevie Wonder
- Valentin Hauy
- American Printing House for the Blind
- The Education for All Children Act of 1975
- Thomas Gallaudet
- National Technical Institute for the Deaf
- Gallaudet University

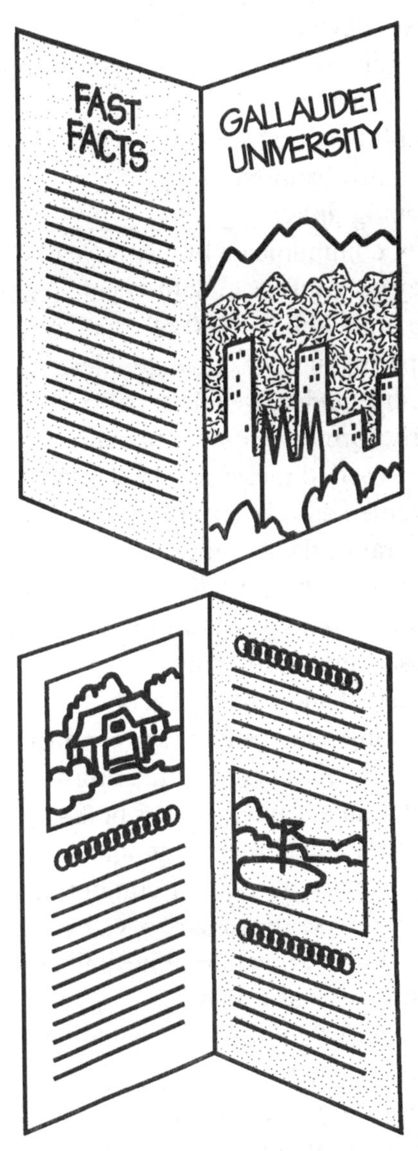

Handy Tip of the Day: *Businesses, organizations, and individuals use brochures to convey messages in a brief format. What are some words that are synonymous with brochure?*

Just for Fun: Imagine that you are running for an elected office. Make a brochure about yourself that will make the voters want to vote for you. Highlight your skills and abilities. Tell about your schooling, hobbies, interests, pets, and other information. Use markers, pens, crayons, or colored pencils to make your brochure attractive to the reader.

Communication Treasure Hunt

REDI* Fill in the blanks by searching through the Treasure Chest for the correct answer.

1. Braille system ____________________
2. first television program in 1928____________________
3. established in 1934 to oversee telephone and telegraph communication ____________________
4. frequency modulation ____________________
5. amplitude modulation ____________________
6. citizen's band radio ____________________
7. cryptography ____________________
8. they communicate by using "calls"____________________
9. they communicate with vocal signals ____________________
10. there are about 3,000 of these in the world today____________________
11. papermaking was invented here in approximately 105 A.D.____________________
12. he invented moveable type from which the Bible was printed ____________________
13. early forms of communication____________________
14. they carried messages through the air ____________________
15. invented a code system of dots and dashes ____________________
16. several of these can pass through the eye of a needle____________________
17. they orbit the earth to provide communication ____________________
18. these were used before the word processors ____________________
19. these can amplify sound ____________________
20. he established the first school for deaf children in 1817____________________
21. this language utilizes signs and finger-spelling____________________
22. these devices can help hearing-impaired people hear ____________________
23. politicians can do this for hours ____________________
24. the first amendment guarantees this right ____________________
25. the primary purpose of communication____________________
26. a lighthouse sends messages by use of this____________________
27. this is also known as a facsimile transmission ____________________
28. also known as e-mail ____________________
29. a singer's "gold record" could be played on this____________________
30. also known as a CD____________________
31. people who break codes____________________
32. writing in picture form____________________
33. Western Union sends these ____________________
34. they had the first telephone conversation ____________________
35. he invented the kinescope ____________________
36. audio visual equipment ____________________
37. it takes your messages when you are not home ____________________
38. they write for newspapers ____________________
39. the world of broadcasting ____________________
40. often needed to pick up signals ____________________

**Research-Explore-Discover-Investigate*

Treasure Chest

antennae
radio, television, magazines, newspapers
journalists
answering machine
overhead projector, filmstrip projector
phonograph
compact disc
a reading system for the blind
FM
AM
CB
birds
whales
languages
China
fax
pictographs and hieroglyphs
smoke, drums, horns
filibuster
to convey messages
pigeons
communication satellites
typewriters
microphone, megaphone
American Sign Language
Free Speech
beacon
cryptographer
telegraphs
Mr. Bell & Mr. Watson
electronic mail
hearing aids
"The Queen's Messenger"
science of communicating by codes
Federal Communication Commission
Johann Gutenberg
Samuel Morse
Thomas Edison
Thomas Gallaudet
fiberoptic cables

Handy Tip of the Day: When you have to read a lot of information and then find answers or select matches as in this activity, plan a strategy (action plan) so that you don't get confused. A strategy for this activity would look like this:

1. Read through everything first and fill in the blanks of things you already know.
2. Cross out Treasure Chest words you have used so that you do not have to keep going over them.
3. Go back over those things you did not know and begin your investigation process using the dictionary, thesaurus, encyclopedia, almanac, computer, or other helpful resource.

*Learning how to find answers is an important skill in school and on the job.

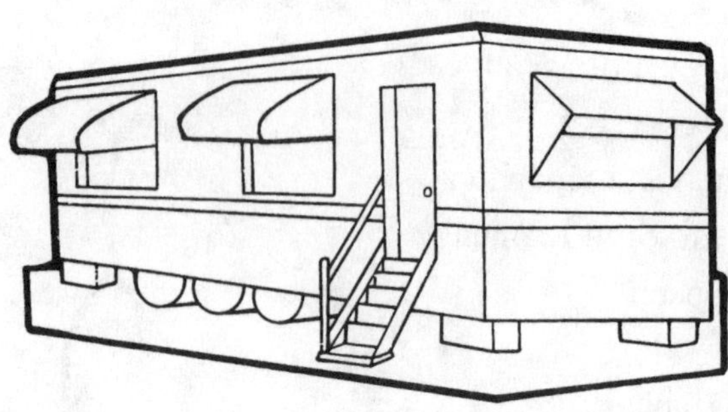

Home and Habitats

Teacher Spin-Off Page

Pre-Writing Discussion Ideas

1. Ask students to think of all the places they have lived. Which home did they like the best?
2. Talk about famous homes—the White House, your state's governor's mansion, British Prime Minister's 10 Downing Street, Buckingham Palace.
3. Gather information about the Biosphere experiment and ask students if they could live in an enclosed habitat for two years.
4. Find information about the space station *Mir* and have students consider what it would be like to live in space for months at a time.
5. Discuss Dorothy and Toto in the *Wizard of Oz* and Dorothy's desire to go home.
6. Talk about the expression "Home is where the heart is." What needs to be present in a dwelling for it to feel like home?
7. Ask students what items they would take if they had to quickly leave their burning home.
8. Compare modest dwellings with lavish dwellings. Ask students which they prefer and why.
9. Ask students if anyone has climbed up to the Swiss Family Robinson Treehouse in Disneyland. Would it be fun to live in a treehouse?

Word Bank Activities

1. Using the word bank, have students make related words (lodging, lodge/shelter, sheltering, etc.).
2. Have students categorize the word bank into the following categories:

   People Dwellings
   Military Dwellings
   Space Dwellings
   Water Dwellings
   Lavish Dwellings
   Religious Dwellings
   Correctional Facility Dwellings
   Animal Dwellings
   Simple Dwellings

3. Have an alphabetizing contest using the word bank and give a simple prize (pencil, eraser top).
4. Divide the class into two teams and have the team recorders at the board. Have teams take turns naming household appliances. The last team to name an appliance is considered the "household champs."
5. Develop further vocabulary by discussing the word "inventory" and talking about the areas in which inventories are used.
6. Have students take a written inventory of their desks. Find out who has the most unusual item.
7. Students can create their own "Minus One-Plus One" game page (See page 116.). Use dark ink and copy each student's game page for each class member. Assemble into packets and have students use as "sponge" activities, or at the beginning of class during roll-taking procedures.
8. Develop a word bank of home styles (Tudor, Cape Cod, colonial, and others) and take a poll to see which style is the most popular.

Teacher Spin-Off Page *(cont.)*

Say It Without Words

1. Use real estate ad booklets to create a collage of different home styles.
2. Create a bulletin board using pictures of homes with different architectural styles.
3. Find pictures of other dwellings from around the world and add them to your board.
4. Provide pictures of the Statue of Liberty and have students sketch the "lady with the golden torch."
5. Collaborate with your music teacher to provide some of the following freedom music of America: "You're a Grand Old Flag," "My Country Tis of Thee," "This Is My Country," "America the Beautiful," "The Star-Spangled Banner," "This Land Is Your Land," etc.
6. Students can illustrate the six animal habitats as individual art projects or they can work together to create a class mural depicting the six habitats.

In The Library

1. Have students do an independent search of an animal and its natural habitat. Give oral presentations.
2. Compile a list of zoos around the world and have students obtain information on the Internet regarding the number of animals in residence and any other information they might find interesting.
3. Students can research animal protection agencies such as Greenpeace and find out what these agencies do to protect and preserve wildlife.
4. Research the topics of animal preserves and animal extinction.
5. Have students assemble a list of animals that are near extinction and animals that are already extinct.

Analytical Lifeskill

1. Have students learn the rules of debate and form debate teams to discuss important issues in the world or in your community.
2. Give students many opportunities to listen to the opinions of their classmates; conversely, give students many opportunities to express their own opinions.
3. Introduce students to the editorial/opinion pages of local papers by reading columns of interest.
4. Have students write letters to the editor voicing their concerns about particular issues.
5. Invite people from the working community to be special speakers on any of the following topics: homebuilding, relief programs, animal rights and safety, genealogy, heritage, immigration.

Answer Key

Page 116 1. refute 2. too 3. pottage 4. save 5. rut 6. eerie 7. furrow 8. ten 9. hike 10. rest 11. tollhouse 12. raven 13. dove 14. page 15. abide 16. rent 17. stack 18. clop 19. stalk 20. scanty

Page 125 1. f 2. aa 3. dd 4. bb 5. cc 6.z 7. y 8. n 9. c 10. a 11. b 12. x 13. d 14. w 15. e 16. v 17. u 18. o 19. q 20. r 21. t 22. s 23. h 24. g 25. k 26. l 27. j 28. i 29. p 30. m

Page 126 Mouse

Word Bank

People and other living creatures live in various types of dwellings. As you read each word, jot down who or what you think might possibly live in each dwelling.

1. domicile ______
2. lodging ______
3. haven ______
4. shelter ______
5. bungalow ______
6. cottage ______
7. cave ______
8. monastery ______
9. cloister ______
10. hut ______
11. townhouse ______
12. condominium ______
13. apartment ______
14. aerie ______
15. burrow ______
16. den ______
17. hive ______
18. nest ______
19. sanctuary ______
20. harbor ______
21. native land ______
22. treehouse ______
23. playhouse ______
24. dollhouse ______
25. boathouse ______
26. cove ______
27. cage ______
28. abode ______
29. abbey ______
30. embassy ______
31. refuge ______
32. biosphere ______
33. residence ______
34. zoo ______
35. cabin ______
36. shack ______
37. mansion ______
38. estate ______
39. tent ______
40. dormitory ______
41. manse ______
42. trailer ______
43. quarters ______
44. billet ______
45. aquarium ______
46. penitentiary ______
47. rest home ______
48. space station ______
49. coop ______
50. stall ______
51. shanty ______
52. hermitage ______
53. barracks ______
54. kennel ______
55. castle ______
56. firehouse ______
57. jail ______
58. palace ______

Minus One, Plus One

If you take one letter away from each of the following words and add another letter, you will form a new word that you can use to fill in the blanks.

- **haven**
- **cottage**
- **cave**
- **hut**
- **aerie**
- **burrow**
- **den**
- **hive**
- **nest**
- **treehouse**
- **native land**
- **cove**
- **cage**
- **abode**
- **refuge**
- **zoo**
- **tent**
- **coop**
- **stall**
- **shanty**
- **dollhouse**

1. I don't want to ______________________ what you have said, but I disagree!
2. The dog wants to go to the park, ______________________ .
3. Did you enjoy eating the ______________________ of meat and vegetables?
4. Please ______________________ a place for me in line.
5. It's good to do something different everyday so that you don't get into a ______________________ .
6. She couldn't sleep after watching the movie last night because it was so______________________ .
7. The tractor made a long ______________________ in the field before planting the seeds.
8. Multiply 9 times 8 then subtract 63 and add 1 to get the number ______________________ .
9. It's always fun to take a ______________________ in the woods.
10. The players were so tired after the game that they took a ______________________.
11. The ______________________ cookie recipe is a favorite for many people.
12. In Edgar Allan Poe's poem "The ______________________," the word "nevermore" is repeated.
13. The symbol for peace is a white ______________________ .
14. You will want to turn the ______________________ in the story to see what happens next.
15. The family decided to stay in the new country and ______________________ there.
16. It is time to pay the ______________________ on the apartment.
17. Should we ______________________ the chairs on top of each other?
18. The horse hooves make a clip-______________________ sound.
19. Put some peanut butter and raisins on a celery ______________________ to make an ant log.
20. Those clothes are too ______________________ for this cold weather.

My Personal Inventory

Now that you are in your new apartment, it's time to get insurance coverage for your personal possessions. You will need to have an inventory of your clothing, appliances, furniture, books, sports equipment, computer equipment and everything else that you want to have the insurance company replace in case of fire or burglary. Itemize your possessions in categories and be sure to include everything of value that you have moved into your apartment.

Furniture

____

____

____

Estimated value: $ ______________

Jewelry

____

____

____

Estimated value: $ ______________

Appliances

____

____

____

Estimated value: $ ______________

Recreational

____

____

____

Estimated value: $ ______________

Clothing

____

____

____

Estimated value: $ ______________

Other

____

____

____

Estimated value: $ ______________

1. Total value of personal inventory (add all of your estimated values): $ ______________
2. My insurance will cover 80% of my losses: (multiply line 1 by .80): $ ______________

Amount I will need to pay for total replacement: (subtract line 2 from line 1): $ ______________

Homeless in America

Today's Reflection: Imagine that you and your family are without a place to live and have no money for housing expenses. You are homeless. Where would you sleep? Where would you bathe and cook? Where would you go after school? Where would you turn for help? Think about the following questions as you write today's reflection.

1. Do you think everyone should have a place to live?

    ____

    ____

2. Besides a place to live, what else does a house provide?

    ____

    ____

3. What do you think is the cause of homelessness in America?

    ____

    ____

4. What kinds of people do you think become homeless?

    ____

    ____

5. What are other problems associated with homelessness?

    ____

    ____

6. If you were able to provide housing for a homeless family, what basic necessities would be supplied for them in their home?

    ____

    ____

Each of these synonyms for "home" means "a safe place"—*shelter, haven, refuge, sanctuary.* Try using these words in your reflection writing. Take notes here during class discussion.

It's Home Improvement Time!

Imagine this! You have been given the opportunity to build your dream house! Get out the hammers, nails, and saw. Put on your tool belt and get busy. As the saying goes, "The sky's the limit!"

Preliminary Planning Worksheet

1. Number of bedrooms ____________________
2. Number of bathrooms ____________________
3. Number of other living areas ____________________
4. List other living areas. ____________________

   ____
5. Number of stories ____________________
6. Garage ____________________
7. Home style ____________________
8. Total number of rooms in your new house: ____________________

Important questions to consider before you start building...

A. Where are you going to build your house?

B. Taking into consideration the weather in the region where you are building, in what month will you begin the work?

C. Describe the style of home you have chosen.

Sketch your initial plan here.

Your Project

Transfer your dream home sketch onto a large piece of construction paper. Include your landscaping ideas and use colored pencils, pens, or crayons to color your plan.

Pioneers and Settlers

Imagine This! In the early days of our country, people moved westward in an attempt to find a place to settle and call home. The pioneers loaded their families and possessions onto horse-drawn wagons and prairie schooners and courageously ventured into unknown territory they had only heard about. There were great risks and dangers ahead for them. However, many of the pioneers were successful in their journeys and found places in which to settle and call home.

Imagine that you and your family have left friends and familiar surroundings to travel to the west for what you have heard will be a better life. You are locating the wagon and must decide what to take and what to leave behind. Your trip will take several weeks and you may find towns with general stores along the way, but there are no guarantees. Careful planning is critical for your survival!

Your packing list:

____

____

____

____

____

____

For further thought:

You and some friends have decided to travel westward to establish a new town. Each of your friends has a specific skill or trade and can make a valuable contribution to this venture. However, there is only room for 10 people on this trip. List the 10 people (by job title) who will go depending on the skills that will be needed the most in your new town.

1. ____
2. ____
3. ____
4. ____
5. ____
6. ____
7. ____
8. ____
9. ____
10. ____

Who Are You Going to Call?

Lifeskill: As you begin the work on your dream home it is important to know the language of the building trade. Look at the words below and write a sentence for each that demonstrates that you know the meaning of the world. Check the dictionary if you need help.

1. contractor We have found a contractor who has agreed to build our house this year.
2. building inspector ____________________
3. designer ____________________
4. architect ____________________
5. plumber ____________________
6. electrician ____________________
7. painter ____________________
8. carpet layer ____________________
9. interior decorator ____________________
10. landscaper ____________________
11. plasterer ____________________
12. excavator ____________________
13. carpenter ____________________
14. bricklayer ____________________
15. cabinet maker ____________________
16. tiler ____________________
17. roofer ____________________

More words to know: Make flashcards with the word on one side and the definition on the other. See how long it takes to put your cards in alphabetical order!

floorplan	**permits**	**exterior**	**plumbing**
interior	**veranda**	**transom**	**bay window**
columns	**master suite**	**stucco**	**blueprints**
fixtures	**specifications**	**excavation**	**utilities**
basement	**foundation**	**septic system**	**roofing**
framing	**insulation**	**decor**	**subfloor**
flooring	**cabinetry**	**switchplates**	**building codes**

Box-Lid House Project

Using your construction paper design plans, build a small-scale house in a box lid. The box lid will enable you to carry and display your house. Use the following specifications for your box-lid house project:

Specifications

- large box lid
- painted scale model house
- full landscaping around entire house

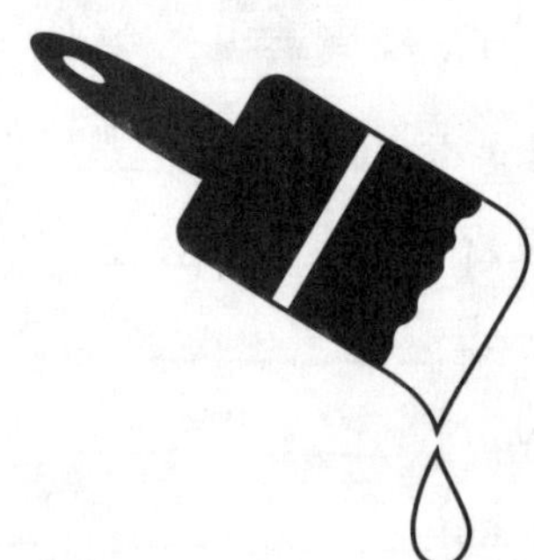

Supplies needed

- small boxes and/or other small containers for house construction
- roofing materials (small pieces of cardboard, wood, etc.)
- paint
- brushes
- sponges (for creating "stucco")
- glue
- landscaping materials—natural: bark, grass, small branches from bushes, small rocks, gravel, sand, etc.; or plastic: legos, etc.

Build your house inside the box lid and glue everything down. Consider other additions such as a swimming pool, gazebo, patio area, picket fence, people or pets.

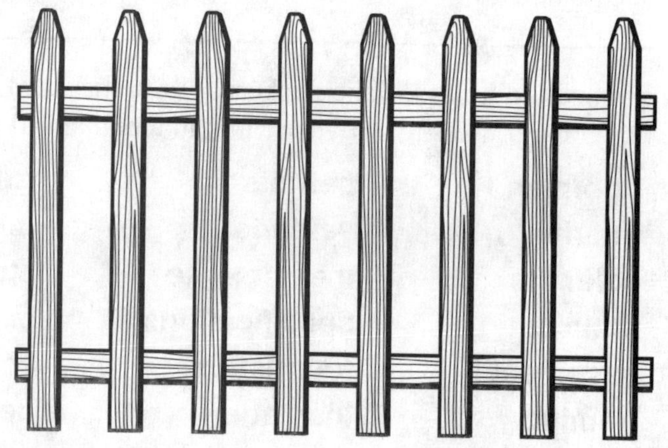

You may also want to attach a backdrop to draw a scene behind your house (mountains, trees, sky, other houses).

Use your imagination and have fun!

Your box lid house project is due on________________.

A Home for the World's Homeless People

Today's Reflection: In 1883 Emma Lazarus wrote the poem "The New Colossus" in honor of the Statue of Liberty. The poem is inscribed on the pedestal of the 151 foot high monument to freedom which was given to the United States of America as a gift from France.

Give me your tired, your poor,
Your huddled masses yearning to breathe free,
The wretched refuse of your teeming shore;
Send these, the homeless, tempest tost to me.
I lift my lamp beside the golden door.

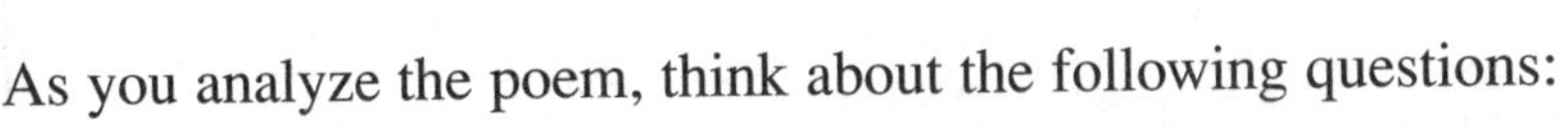

As you analyze the poem, think about the following questions:

1. Who is the voice in this poem? Who is speaking? ____________
2. Who are the "tired" and "poor"? ____________
3. What are the "huddled masses"? ____________
4. Why are they "yearning to breathe free"? ____________
5. Who or what has taken away their freedom? ____________
6. Why would people be referred to as "wretched refuse"? ____________
7. Why are these people homeless? ____________
8. What is the "lamp" and what does it symbolize? ____________
9. What is the "golden door"? ____________
10. What does the "golden door" symbolize? ____________

For further reflection: People around the world become "homeless" because of war, political, religious, or racial persecution, or economic upheaval. During our nation's history, many people have looked to America as a land rich in freedom, opportunity, and hope. However, in recent years, laws have been enacted making the "golden door" difficult to open for many people. Write an opinion paper stating your thoughts on the "golden door" and America being a "home" for the world's "homeless."

Which Way Is Home?

Analytical Lifeskill: In the film *The Wizard of Oz*, which is based on the famous book by Frank Baum, Dorothy finds herself in another world far from home. She searches desperately for a way to go home but can't find her way. In the end, Dorothy clicks her heels together and repeats the words "There's no place like home, there's no place like home" and finds herself reunited with her beloved family and home.

For you to do: Make a map from school to your home. Put in stop signs, lights, intersections, key buildings and structures, and anything else that will help you get home!

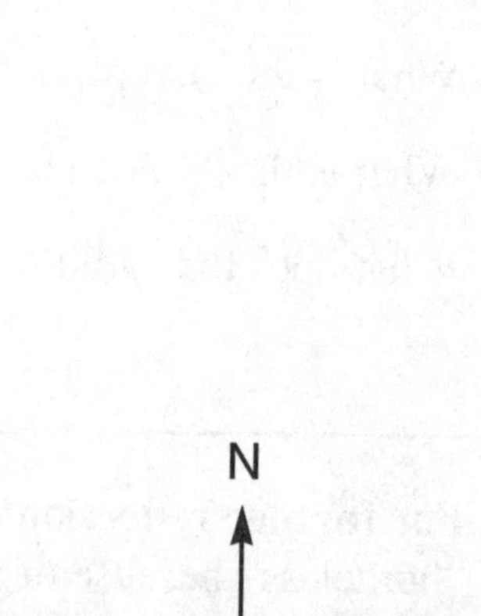

N

W E

S

A Step Further: Try your hand at writing clear directions for getting to school from your home.

What Are You Really Trying to Say?

Let's Talk About It: There are many "old sayings" that people have used to express an idea or sentiment. These expressions are called idioms. You have been given the beginning of each idiom or idiomatic expression. Now see if you can finish it. On the long blank line, write the words that will complete the phrase; on the short line, write the letter corresponding to the correct phrase. Just put your shoulder to the wheel and your nose to the grindstone and you will find that you are as sharp as a tack!

______ 1. fish or ______________________
______ 2. like a fish out ______________________
______ 3. we have other fish ______________________
______ 4. home is where you hang ______________________
______ 5. something up ______________________
______ 6. between a rock and a ______________________
______ 7. take the bull ______________________
______ 8. working without a ______________________
______ 9. let sleeping ______________________
______ 10. a bone ______________________
______ 11. the sky's the ______________________
______ 12. don't bite the hand ______________________
______ 13. don't look a gift horse ______________________
______ 14. eat you out of house ______________________
______ 15. in one ear ______________________
______ 16. a bird in the hand is worth ______________________
______ 17. straight from the horse's ______________________
______ 18. without a leg ______________________
______ 19. look before ______________________
______ 20. went over like a ______________________
______ 21. out on a ______________________
______ 22. wear your heart ______________________
______ 23. sick to my ______________________
______ 24. born with a silver ______________________
______ 25. turn over a ______________________
______ 26. sink or ______________________
______ 27. take a flying ______________________
______ 28. take to it like a duck to ______________________
______ 29. tighten your ______________________
______ 30. left holding the ______________________

a. to pick
b. limit
c. dogs lie
d. in the mouth
e. and out the other
f. cut bait
g. spoon in his/her mouth
h. stomach
i. water
j. leap
k. new leaf
l. swim
m. bag
n. net
o. to stand on
p. belt
q. you leap
r. lead balloon
s. on your sleeve
t. limb
u. mouth
v. two in the bush
w. and home
x. that feeds you
y. by the horns
z. a hard place
aa. of water
bb. your hat
cc. your sleeve
dd. to fry

For further thought: Why do you think people use idioms and idiomatic expressions?

House and Home Word Tag

Find each of the following highlighted words in the word tag game below. Each word is connected to another word, and words can be found in all directions.

White House, House of **Representatives**, House of **Lords**, House of **Commons**, Home **Sweet** Home, **Homestead** Act, Housing and **Urban** Development, **Opera** House, House of **Worship**, **Brokerage** House, **Homestyle** Cooking, Home **Town**, House **Arrest**, Home on the **Range**, **Homecoming**, House at **Pooh** Corner, Little House on the **Prairie**.

Write the five unused bold-faced letters on the line below. Unscramble the letters to learn what you do not want in your home.

_____ _____ _____ _____ _____ A_______________________!

D	B	A	G	I	R	V	H	K	J	Z	B	D	H	A	Q
W	R	C	F	K	U	R	B	A	N	L	P	O	**M**	R	A
H	O	M	E	S	T	E	A	D	Y	O	O	C	U	I	E
I	K	E	**U**	S	C	P	X	I	O	P	E	K	D	N	C
T	E	H	Q	L	O	R	D	S	W	E	E	T	S	F	H
E	R	S	C	J	M	E	G	L	P	R	A	I	R	I	E
L	A	W	**O**	W	M	S	V	X	B	A	R	R	E	S	T
P	G	M	T	D	O	E	R	M	P	F	G	A	I	M	J
B	E	T	X	J	N	N	U	Q	W	A	D	N	E	C	F
N	H	O	M	E	S	T	Y	L	E	I	G	G	A	Q	Z
Y	I	W	**E**	G	X	A	P	U	C	J	B	E	G	C	P
K	A	N	D	E	B	T	**S**	R	I	H	H	D	R	B	M
P	W	O	R	S	H	I	P	V	K	N	M	R	Q	A	R
Q	Z	L	F	R	T	V	T	L	P	J	O	D	L	F	B
M	A	Y	H	O	M	E	C	O	M	I	N	G	C	S	E
O	S	C	E	N	D	S	M	Q	A	S	E	D	T	C	B

Habitats: Natural and Unnatural

Say It Without Words: Although most of the world's wild animals live in their natural habitats, there are many animals that live in captivity in people-created environments.

For your thinking...

Consider: Many animals live in zoos. Even though modern zoos, or zoological gardens, have tried to simulate the animal's natural habitat or environment, can this be home?

Consider: Many animals live in cages and travel with the circus. Can this be home?

Consider: Many large sea animals live in aquariums. Can this be home?

Consider: Some people have very strong feelings about the educational value of making wild animals accessible to the public. Other people have strong feelings against keeping wild animals in captivity. What do you think? Should animals be allowed to remain free in their natural habitats, or should people be allowed to capture them and place them in unnatural habitats?

For you to do: Without using words, make a poster that illustrates your position.

Brainstorm your thoughts by making a list of contrasting arguments.

Reasons to Keep Animals in Captivity	Reasons to Free Animals From Captivity

It's Home To Me

Animals live in six natural habitats throughout the world. Read the description of each habitat and then place each animal from the Creatures Great and Small box in its proper habitat.

Polar Region
(arctic ice and arctic tundra—COLD!)

Grassland and Prairies
(wide-open expanse of land)

Desert
(very hot, very dry, little rain)

Mountains
(multi-leveled/snowy peaks, cliffs, plateaus, valleys)

Ocean and Shore
(water, water everywhere rocks, sand, reefs)

Forest
(plants, trees, foliage, rain)

Creatures Great and Small

skunk, tiger, monkey, porcupine, lion, aardvark, kangaroo, grizzly bear, fox, polar bear, fish, yak, birds, octopus, clam, sting ray, camel, kangaroo rat, snake, leopard, tarantula, exotic birds ape, whale, sea lion, crab, zebra, giraffe, ostrich, sheep, goats, loon, lemming, caribou, bat, lizard, mule deer, coyote, shark, sea urchin, hawk, raccoon, tiger, hippopotamus, elephant, prairie dog, penguin, ermine, snowy owl, vulture

Appendix

Ready-to Use Communications

Student Master Pages

Supply Wish List

Dear Parents,

During the school year, our class will be creating various art projects to accompany our language arts lessons. Your help is needed to put together an arts and crafts supply center for our classroom. Many of the items that we need may be found in your closets, cupboards, workshops, and garages. Please let me know if you think of any other useful supplies that are not on the list.

Thank you for your help as we work together to make this a great learning year!

Sincerely,

____

Supply Wish List

- fabric pieces
- yarn
- ribbon
- thread (embroidery, sewing)
- leather scraps
- small blocks of wood
- beads
- wallpaper samples
- contact paper
- felt
- small pieces of cardboard
- string
- aluminum foil
- gold foil
- garden magazines
- fabric paint
- glitter
- sequins
- plastic bags that zipper lock (to store small individual projects)
- new sponges (cut into squares for sponge painting)
- gift wrap scraps
- art tissue paper
- crepe paper
- shoe boxes for storage
- magazines (gardening, nature/outdoor, animals, food, travel, youth)
- greeting card pictures
- travel brochures
- other____________________________

Wish List Memo

To: Parents and Staff

Date:____________________

From:____________________

Regarding: Magazine Collection for Classroom Library

Dear Parents and Staff,

I am assembling a classroom library of magazines that will be useful to my students as they explore a variety of topics (see the list below). Would you consider recycling your magazines by donating them to my class? Thank you in advance for your helpfulness!

Topics

- seasons/weather
- transportation/travel
- hopes/dreams
- insects/bugs
- exploration/adventure
- pets/friends
- homes/habitats
- communications/connections

Magazines Needed

National Geographic (and other travel titles)

Smithsonian

Outdoor Life (and other outdoor titles)

Popular Mechanics

Car & Driver (and other auto titles)

Architectural Digest

Sunset

Sports Illustrated (and other sports titles)

Also, magazines about pets, animals, food, nutrition, science, technology, gardening

Parent Survey

From The Desk of ______________________________

Dear Parents,

I want you to know about some of the enrichment units we will be enjoying this year. I would also like to enlist your expertise and experience whenever possible.

Look at the selected topics and let me know if you are available to participate in any way.

Thank you for considering sharing your knowledge and abilities with our class!

- Seasons and Weather
- Transportation and Travel
- Hopes and Dreams (education, career, family life)
- Insects and Bugs
- Exploration and Adventure
- Pets and Friends
- Homes and Habitats
- Communication and Connections

____
Teacher

Please circle and return to school

Yes. I can be a special speaker during your unit on ______________________.
Contact me about a specific date.

No. I cannot be a special speaker, but I know someone who would be knowledgeable in one of the units.______________________________

Yes. I can help with special art/craft projects.

My name:

____

My child's name:

____

My phone number: ______________________________

Say It Without Words

Name: ______________________________ Date: ____________________

Today's Reflection

Topic: ____

____

____

____

____

____

____

____

____

____

____

____

____

____

____

____

____

Create a Crossword

Use the words from the word bank and the worksheet below to make a crossword puzzle. Here is how to do it.

1. Choose one word from the word bank list, and write it on the grid.
2. Choose a second word that shares at least one letter with the first word and add it to the grid.
3. Continue until you have used 10 or more words. Check to make sure that all adjacent letters form words.
4. Number the words in the puzzle. Number one is the word whose first letter is closest to the top left corner of the grid. Continue numbering across the top row. Move to the next row and continue numbering from left to right.
5. On a separate grid, outline the letter boxes and number them.
6. Below the blank puzzle, list the numbers of the words that go across and the numbers of words that go down.
7. Write a clue for each of the words, using complete sentences. Your clues may be definitions, synonyms, or sentences with a blank where the word should go.
8. Exchange puzzles with a classmate and solve them.

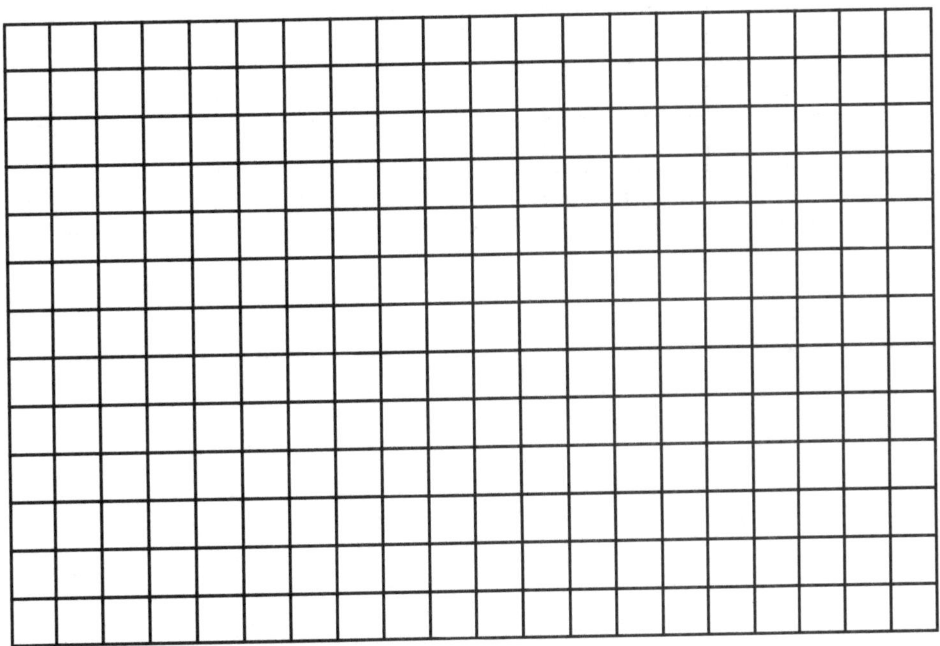

Across

____

____

____

____

____

Down

____

____

____

____

____

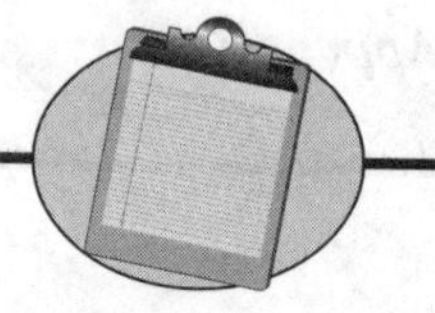

Make a Word Search

Use 20 words from your word bank or writer's workshop writings to create your own word search. Make a list of the words you will include in your puzzle on the lines provided. Use capital letters and a dark pen to write your words backwards, forwards, diagonally, vertically, or horizontally. Leave spaces between your words. When you have placed your words where you want them, fill in the blanks starting with letter "A" and moving through the alphabet until you have filled all of the spaces.

Calendar for the Month of ____________

Sunday	Monday	Tuesday	Wednesday	Thursday	Friday	Saturday

Daily Schedule

Name______________________________ Day______________ Date________________

	Activity
7 a.m.	
8 a.m.	
9 a.m.	
10 a.m.	
11 a.m.	
12 p.m.	
1 p.m.	
2 p.m.	
3 p.m.	
4 p.m.	
5 p.m.	
6 p.m.	
7 p.m.	
8 p.m.	
9 p.m.	
10 p.m.	

Extra, Extra, Read All About It!

Name:____________________________________ Date: __________________________

Use this form to submit a mini-report on any subject that interests you. You may earn extra points as well as gain extra knowledge in your selected topic.

A. Topic Title:

B. Your Source(s) of Information:

1. ____

2. ____

C. Write a synopsis (summary) of the information you have found. You must use your own words. Copying from a reference book or other source is called *plagiarism* and cannot be accepted. Trust your own words—they are good, too!

D. What do you find particularly interesting about this topic? ____________________

E. Would you like to learn more about this topic? ____________________________

F. What is your synopsis word count? If you are doing your synopsis on a computer, you can get an automatic word count and spelling check from the tool bar.

Ready Report Reference

The Title Page

A formal report begins with a title page, which gives important information about the report. The basic questions to be answered on the title page are:

1. What is it about?	*title of the paper*
2. Who wrote it?	*name of the author*
3. For whom was it written?	*name of the teacher who assigned it*
4. What is its purpose?	*subject or class in which it was assigned*
5. When was it written?	*date*
6. Where was it written?	*name of the school (optional)*

Look at the examples below to see how the information is arranged on the page. Ask before including artwork on your title page.

The History of Human Powered Flight

by Alice Brown

Social Studies, Period 4

Mr. Monteros

April 10, 1999

Ocean Life

by Alex Sandoval

English, Period 6

Mrs. Martin

Jefferson Middle School January 15, 1998

Ready Report Reference *(cont.)*

The Bibliography

The bibliography is the last page of any report. It gives information about the sources you used in creating your document. When you are doing your research, make sure that you copy all the information about the source: title, author, publisher, volume (if given), and date of publication for each reference.

To make a bibliography, list your sources alphabetically by the author's last name. If no author is given, place the title in the correct alphabetical sequence (skip *a*, *an*, and *the*).

Your bibliography entries will be single spaced, with a space between entries. The first line is flush with the left margin, but the all lines after the first are indented five spaces. On the computer, this is called a "hanging indent." If you handwrite your report, underline any titles. For a report done on a computer, italicize the titles. Refer to the examples below for correct order and punctuation. Use a period after the author, the title, and the date.

Books

(one author)

Baum, Frank L. *The Wizard of Oz*. Rand McNally & Co., 1956.

(two or more authors)

Bradley, James and Mary Ryan. *There's No Place Like Home*. McMillan Publishing Co., 1992.

(edited book)

Burns, Richard S., ed. *Home is Where the Heart Is*. Random House, 1989.

Encyclopedia Articles

(no author listed)

"Home Construction." *World Book Encyclopedia*. (21st ed., 1992), IV, 425 ff.

(author listed)

Charleston, Daniel. "Africa." *World Book Encyclopedia*, 1980.

Internet

(article in a reference database)

"Fresco." *Britannica Online*. Vers. 97.1.1. Mar. 1997. *Encyclopaedia Britannica*. 29 Mar. 1997 http://www.eb.com/180.

(Webpage)

Hixson, Susan. *Internet in the Classroom* [Online]. http://www.indirect.com/www/dhixson/class.html

Mapquest. http://www.mapquest.com.

Information on CD-ROM

The CIA World Factbook. CD-ROM. Minneapolis: Quanta, 1992.

Magazine or Newspaper

Miller, Diana. "How to Find Your Way Anywhere." *Saturday Evening Post*, September, 1991, 56–58.

Video and Television

Animal Homes. A National Geographic Production. Fort Collins, CO, 1993.

"The Blessing Way." *The X-Files*. Fox. WXIA, Atlanta. 19 Jul. 1998.

Student/Teacher "PERC" (Personal Evaluation/Response Communication)

To: (*insert your name here*) ____________________

From: (*insert student's name*) ____________________

For unit: (*unit title*) ____________________

Date: ____________

1. What would you like me to notice most about your unit folder?
2. What activity did you enjoy the most and why?
3. What activity did you least enjoy and why?
4. Tell me one or two things that you learned during the unit that were interesting to you.
5. Would you like more information about anything in this unit?
6. Evaluate your work by putting an **x** in the box that most applies.

   ❑ I think this is some of my best work.

   ❑ I put as much effort into my folder as I could have.

   ❑ I know I could improve the quality of my unit folder.

Circle your final self-assessment of your work.

Excellent *Very Good* *Moderately Good*

Needs Improvement *Incomplete*

Teacher's Comments . . .

____

____

____

____

____

(Personalize this section. Consider varying your response mode—use a checklist style for some units and personal narrative evaluation for others according to your students' needs and your time.)

Useful URLs

The Internet is a major source of information on a variety of topics. Sites on the Internet change daily, as new web pages are added and others move or are deleted. The following list of sites is current as of the date of publication. Use the suggested keywords, or your own words and phrases, with any web browser to explore the Internet for other sites.

Note to teacher: You may wish to install a filtering program like *WebSense* or *Surf Watch* before students begin searching on their own.

My Favorite Season

http://www.awc-kc.noaa.gov/wxfact.html
http://www.disasterrelief.org/
http://www.aoml.noaa.gov/general/lib/hurricbro.html
Keywords: hurricanes, weather, blizzard, climate

Transportation and Travel

http://aeroweb.brooklyn.cuny.edu/history/wright/wright.html
http://news.courant.com/news/special/amelia/links.stm
http://www.encyberpedia.com/aviation.htm
Keywords: bicycle, dog sled, airplanes, public transit, trains

Hopes and Dreams

http://www.uhs.berkeley.edu/careerlibrary/links/careerme.htm
Keywords: careers, education

Bugs and Insects

http://www.ufsia.ac.be/Arachnology/Arachnology.html
http://www.ex.ac.uk/bugclub/
Keywords: spiders, bugs, insects, pest control

Exploration and Adventure

http://www.biography.com/
Keywords: use names of individuals, specific locations, etc.

Pets and Friends

http://www.purina.com/
http://freezone.com/kclub/purfpets/petintro.html
http://www.acmepet.com/
http://www.bcyellowpages.com/advert/b/BCHES/petshome.htm
Keywords: dogs, cats, pets, reptiles

Homes and Habitats

http://www.uniteddesign.com/
http://www.hcs.ohio-state.edu/hcs/WebGarden.html
http://www.hoptechno.com/book26.htm
Keywords: home design, gardening, plants, vegetables

Communication and Connections

http://www.eb.com/alpha/lists.htcl?aDB=biog_alpha&nHits=10&mode=4
http://www.s9.com/biography/index.html
http://www.mediahistory.com/
Keywords: media, history of television, technology

General Resources:

Internet Public Library

Word Search and Word Tag Answer Keys

Page 13 My Favorite Season Word Search

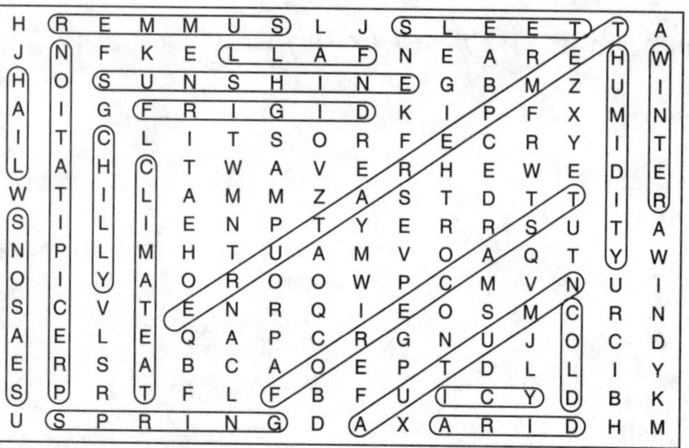

Page 56 Bug Search

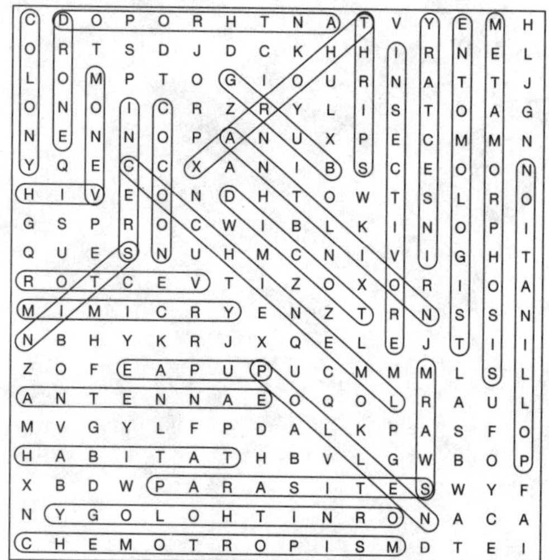

Page 78 Adventures in Literature and Film

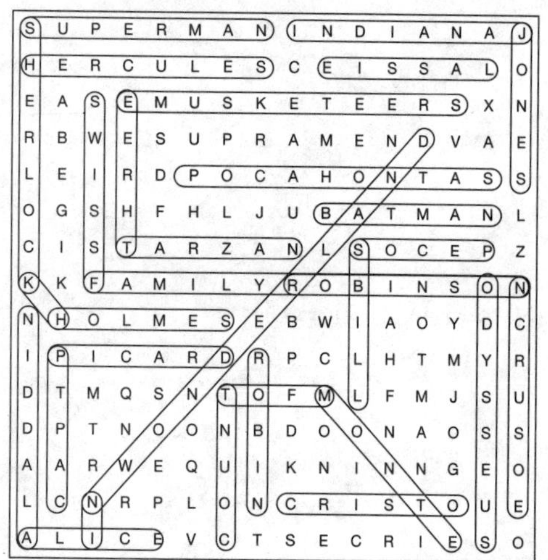

Page 87 Aquarium Fish Find

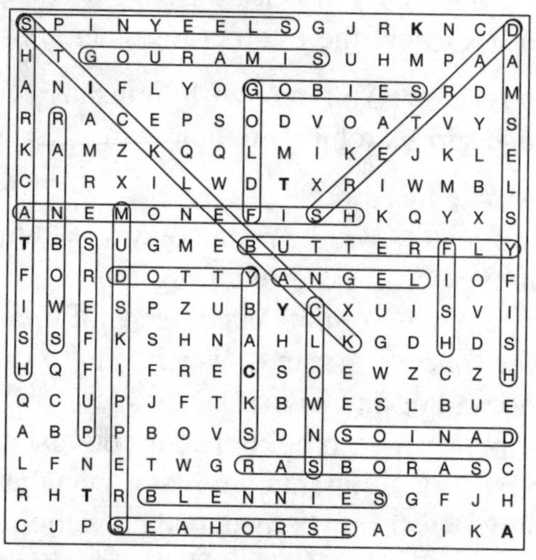

Page 103 Communications Tools Word Search

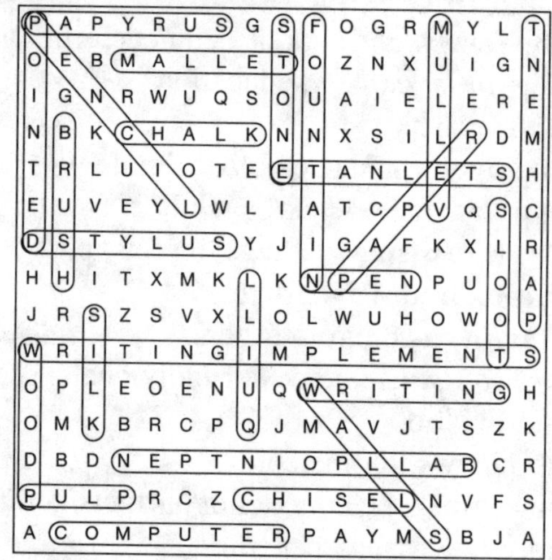

Page 126 House and Home Word Tag

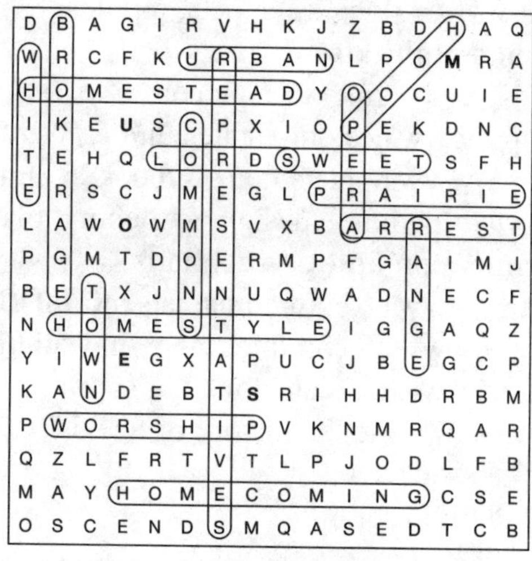

